The Life of
Captain Alonso de Contreras

Knight of the Military Order of
St. John, Native of Madrid
Written by Himself
(1582 to 1633)

Translated from the Spanish
by
Catherine Alison Phillips
With an Introduction by
David Hannay

New York
Alfred A. Knopf

MADE & PRINTED IN GREAT BRITAIN
BY BUTLER & TANNER LTD
FROME AND
LONDON

SEA-FIGHT BETWEEN MALTESE GALLEYS AND TURKISH SHIPS, BY GASPAR VAN EYCK

(Madrid, Prado)

[*Frontispiece*

Contents

CHAP.   PAGE

I   OF MY INFANCY AND PARENTAGE   11

II   OF WHAT HAPPENED UP TO MY SECOND RETURN TO MALTA   21

III   OF WHAT HAPPENED UP TO THE MIRACLE OF THE ISLE OF LAMPEDUSA   32

IV   IN WHICH ARE CONTINUED MY VOYAGES IN THE LEVANT AND WHAT CAME TO PASS UNTIL I CAME TO THE ISLAND OF ESTAMPALIA   48

V   WHICH CONTINUES TILL THE TIME WHEN I CAME TO MALTA AGAIN FROM THE LEVANT   64

VI   IN WHICH IS RELATED HOW I WENT FORTH FROM MALTA AND BETOOK MYSELF TO SPAIN, WHERE I BECAME AN ENSIGN   91

VII   IN WHICH ARE CONTINUED MY ADVENTURES AS AN ENSIGN   104

VIII   IN WHICH IS RELATED THE LOSS OF THE LORD GOVERNOR OF CASTILLE AT LA MAHOMETA, WHERE I WAS PRESENT   118

IX   HOW I WENT TO SPAIN AND THERE WAS FALSELY ALLEGED TO BE KING OF THE MORISCOES, WHICH CAUSED ME MUCH TRAVAIL   131

X   IN WHICH IS CONTINUED THE COLLECTION OF EVIDENCE ABOUT WHO WAS KING   146

[1]

CONTENTS

CHAP.   PAGE

XI   IN WHICH IS RELATED THE DEPARTURE
WHICH I MADE FROM MADRID FOR
FLANDERS AND WHAT HAPPENED AT
THE DEATH OF THE KING OF FRANCE   164

XII   HOW, BEING COME TO MALTA, I RE-
TURNED TO SPAIN AND BECAME A
CAPTAIN IN THE SPANISH INFANTRY,
WITH OTHER EVENTS   182

XIII   IN WHICH IS RELATED THE VOYAGE I
MADE TO THE INDIES, AND WHAT
CAME TO PASS THERE   196

XIV   HOW I RELIEVED THE FORCES AT LA
MÁMORA, AND OTHER HAPPENINGS   206

XV   HOW I RAISED ANOTHER COMPANY OF
INFANTRY IN MADRID AT ANTÓN
MARTÍN, AND OTHER HAPPENINGS   218

XVI   ARRIVAL OF THE MARQUIS OF CADREYTA
AT ROME. ERUPTION OF VESUVIUS. MY
STAY AT THE CASALES OF CAPUA. MY
GOVERNORSHIP OF THE CITY OF AQUILA   231

XVII   OF DIVERS THINGS WHICH HAPPENED TO
ME IN CAPUA. IN PRAISE OF THE
COUNT AND COUNTESS OF MONTEREY.
I RETIRE FROM THEIR SERVICE   249

XVIII   VOYAGES TO NAPLES, GENOA, AND SPAIN.
MY BROTHER'S PRETENSIONS   268

APPENDIX I   275

APPENDIX II   281

APPENDIX III   286

[2]

Illustrations

FACING
PAGE

FRONTISPIECE: Sea-fight between Maltese
galleys and Turkish ships, by Gaspar van
Eyck (Madrid, Prado)

PHILIBERT, PRINCE OF ONEGLIA, grandson of
Emmanuel Philibert of Savoy, and afterwards Viceroy of Sicily, where Van Dyck
painted this portrait (London, Dulwich
Gallery)   25

ALOF DE VIGNACOURT, Grand Master of the
Order of St. John of Jerusalem from
1601–1621. Portrait by Caravaggio (Paris,
Louvre)   41

TURKISH CARAMUZAL IN ACTION. From J.
Fürttenbach, *Architectura navalis* (1629)   59

A MALTESE GALLEY, flying the standard of the
Grand Master, drawn by Antonio Borg
(British Museum, Dept. of MSS.)   80

PHILIP III OF SPAIN. Portrait by Velazquez
(Madrid, Prado)   131

THE INFANTA ISABELLA CLARA EUGENIA in
the habit of the Poor Clares. Portrait by
Rubens, engraved by Paul Pontius (B.M.
Print Room)   165

SIR WALTER RALEIGH. Portrait by Zucchero
(London, National Portrait Gallery)   197

[3]

ILLUSTRATIONS

FACING
PAGE

YOUTHFUL PORTRAIT OF PHILIP IV OF SPAIN,
by Velazquez (Madrid, Prado)   211

LOPE FELIX DE VEGA CARPIO, wearing the
habit of the Order of St. John of Jerusalem
(From a print in the B.M.)   223

DON MANUEL DE ACEBEDO Y ZÚÑIGA, 6TH
COUNT OF MONTEREY, Viceroy of Naples
(From a print in the B.M.)   233

DON ALVARO DE BAZÁN Y BENAVIDES, 2ND
MARQUIS OF SANTA CRUZ (1571–1664).
Portrait by Van Dyck, engraved by Pontius
(B.M. Print Room)   273

Translator's Note

The translator desires to express her obligation to Mr. G. E. Manwaring for kindly placing at her disposal his expert knowledge of naval history, and reading the manuscript in order to ensure that the nautical details should be correct.

Introduction

At all times, and mostly when she was at her best, Spain has been the fertile mother of two types of man: the 'Señor Soldado' and the 'Picaro.' We are not to assume hastily that the first is just a Good Soldier, or that the second is a Mere Rogue. Careful selection and intensive training are needed to make a disciplined man of the Spaniard. By nature he is a champion, a guerrillero, and a seeker of El Dorado. As for the Picaro, he has made use of roguery, but there has ever been in him an element of African nomad, herdsman of migratory herds, an Ishmael who wanders because he needs must, having the vagabond in his blood. So it was ages before the Phœnicians planted a trading post at Cadiz about 1000 B.C. Africa begins at the Pyrenees. There have been invasions from Europe, and great European influences have been at work – the Latin Language, the Roman Law, and the Catholic Apostolic Church – not without results. But the foundation is African.

Since the Señor Soldado was much of a partisan, and fighter for his own hand, and the Picaro was in good part a Bedoween, what was more natural than

[6]

that they should be combined in one hero? Mrs.
Phillips has earned the sincere thanks of readers of
English from both sides of borders and oceans by
presenting them with this translation of the memoirs
of a fine specimen of the kind, the Captain Alonso
de Contreras. Mrs. Phillips, too, has been so kind,
and so truly critical, as not to write her version in a
language which is not the English of our day, in the
vain hope of finding an equivalent for the Castilian
of the seventeenth century. Wardour Street lies
that way, and, moreover, you may hear Alonso's
vocabulary and his syntax in Madrid or Toledo
whenever you like, and still more certainly at
Almonacid de Zorita, or Egea de los Caballeros.
Nor will Alonso be lacking in the flesh if you look
for him. If the Spaniard does not now shine before
our eyes as he once did, the reason is not that he has
altered, but that the world has. The occasion no
longer fits the virtue – or when it did for a few
years in the Peninsular War there was Alonso de
Contreras in the persons of Chapalangarra, the
Empecinado – and many another guerrillero, who
among them saved the honour of Spain when her
politicians and regular soldiers failed.

There is no doubt of the authenticity of the

memoirs published by Señor Serrano y Sanz and
translated by Mrs. Phillips. The MSS. is preserved.
We have the word of Lope de Vega for Alonso and
his reputation in his lifetime. Besides, there are the
official documents Mrs. Phillips prints in the Appendix to confirm his evidence as given for himself.
Best testimony of all is the obvious veracity of his
narrative. There is no danger in taking him as he
drew himself. The very candour with which this
man, who yet valued his reputation after a sort,
records how he began by murdering a fellow-school-
boy, how he enlisted, and was easily led to desert,
how he wandered and adventured in cruises in the
Levant and tavern brawls, how he took care to provide for himself by pillaging a prize, speaks for him.
He did not repent – not a bit of it. The adventures
befell him, and he saw no sin in what came to him
by fortune. So he may be believed when he tells
how he was always well to the front with sword,
buckler and javelin and arquebus, warring from the
Levant to the Antilles, where he had a brush at long
bowls with the ships of 'Guaterral,' whom we know
as Sir Walter Raleigh, on their way home from that
sad business in Guiana; then from the Antilles to
Flanders, and again to Naples, and the Order of St.

INTRODUCTION

John; how he squandered his booty on daughters of
the horse-leech; married and killed his wife with her
lover; saw great men and found the Court a snare
and a delusion; how he was a good Christian but did
not scruple to pretend for business reasons to be a
hermit. The underlying scepticism and irreverence
of his kind oozes out now and then. Incidentally
he lets us see the growing anarchy of Spain in
the seventeenth century, and such examples of its
unwisdom as the expulsion of the Moriscoes. Of
course he once got into trouble with the law and
was racked. The reader will see how and why, and
believe him, for Alonso de Contreras has left an
historic document of real value as well as a revelation
from the inside of the quintessential – Señor Soldado
and Picaro.

DAVID HANNAY.

The story of my life, from the time I went forth to serve the King, being fourteen years of age, which was in the year 1595, till the end of the year 1630, on the first of October, when I began this narrative.

The Life of Captain
Alonso de Contreras

Chapter i

Of my Infancy and Parentage

∽

I WAS born in the most noble city of Madrid, on JANUARY 6, 1582. I was baptized in the parish church of San Miguel. My god-parents were Alonso de Roa and María de Roa, my mother's brother and sister. My parents' names were Gabriel Guillén and Juana de Roa y Contreras. I desired to take my mother's surname when I went as a boy to serve the King, and by the time I was aware of the mistake I had made, I could not undo it; for my name had gone down in my service papers as Contreras, and under that name I have passed unto this day; and by this name I am known, notwithstanding that in my baptism they called me Alonso de Guillén; and I call myself Alonso de Contreras. My parents were Old Christians, with no blood of Moor or Jew, nor had they been punished by the Holy Office. As

[11]

will be seen in the course of this narration, they were
poor, and lived in the married state, as Holy Mother
Church commands, for four-and-twenty years,
during which time they had seventeen children.
When my father died there were eight remaining –
six men-children and two females – and I was the
eldest of all. At the time when my father died I was
going to school and writing a large round hand; and
at this time lists were laid out for jousting in Madrid
on one side of the Segovian Bridge, where they
were wont to pitch tents; and all the town went out
to see it as some new thing. I joined another boy,
the son of an alguacil of the court, whose name was
Salvador Moreno, and we went off to see the joust,
playing truant from school. On the morrow, when
I went back, the master told me to step up and untruss another boy, for, said he, he considered me
a brave fellow. I stepped up with a will, and the
master behind me. But he had laid a trap for me;
for he ordered me to untruss myself, and laid on
with a parchment rod till he drew blood. This was
done at the instance of the boy's father, who was
richer than mine. On leaving school, as was my
habit, I went off with this boy to the *plaza* by the
Hieronimite Church of the Conception; and being

still in pain from the rod, I drew out my knife from my writing-case and, flinging the boy down with his face to the ground, I began to stab him with my penknife. And since it seemed to me that I was not hurting him, I turned him over face uppermost and stabbed him in the belly. All the boys said that I had killed him, so I made off; and at night I went home as if I had done nothing. On that day we were short of bread, so my mother had given each of us a penny cake. As I was eating it there came a violent knocking at the door; and when we asked who was there, they answered, 'The Law.' Upon this I went up to the top of the house and got under my mother's bed. The alguacil came in and looked for me. He found me, and, dragging me out with a turn of the hand, he said, 'Traitor, it is thou who hast slain my son!' They took me to the court-house gaol, where they took down my statement. I steadily denied everything, and on the morrow they examined me with twenty-two other boys whom they had taken up. When the clerk of the court read out the story of how I had stabbed the boy with the knife in my writing-case, I said it was not so, but that another boy had struck him; upon which all we boys came to blows in the court before the judge, each one maintaining that another had struck the blow. And it was with no small ado that they pacified us and threw us out of the hall. To make a long story short, the father set to work with such a will, that in two days he proved that I was guilty. On account of my tender years opinions were divided, but in the end I was saved by the fact of being a minor, and they sentenced me to a year's banishment five leagues away from the court, which I was not to infringe under pain of double banishment. So I set out forthwith to carry it into effect. But the alguacil remained bereft of his son, for he died two days after.

I passed my year of banishment at Ávila in the house of an uncle of mine, who was priest of the parish of St. James's (Santiago) in that city; and at the end of it I returned to Madrid. Within twenty days of my arrival there came thither the Cardinal Archduke Albert, who had left the governorship of Portugal and was on his way to govern the Flemish provinces. My mother had divided up our fortune and withdrawn her marriage-portion. There remained 600 reals to be divided among all us eight brothers. And thus I spoke to my mother, 'Madam,

I would go to the wars with the Cardinal.' And she said to me, 'Child, you are not out of your shell, and you wish to go to the wars! I have just apprenticed you to the craft of a silversmith.' I said I had no mind to follow a craft, but the King. But notwithstanding she took me to the house of the silversmith, having arranged it without my consent. She left me at his house. And the first thing my mistress did was to give me a copper pitcher, and that no small one, and send me with it for water to the Peartree Spring. I said to her that I had not come to be a servant, but to learn a craft, and that she might send whom she pleased to fetch the water. She lifted up her clog to strike me, and I up with the pitcher and flung it at her, though I could do her no hurt, for I was not strong enough; and I rushed away down the stairs and was off to my mother's house, crying aloud, 'Why should I go and serve as a water-carrier?' Upon this the silversmith came up and wanted to thrash me. I went outside and loaded myself with stones and began to stone him; on which the neighbours gathered round and, having heard what was to do, they asked why I should be compelled against my will. So the silversmith departed, and I remained with my mother, to whom

I said, 'Madam, your worship is weighed down with children. Let me go and seek my livelihood with this Prince.' And my mother made up her mind to it, but said, 'I have nothing to give you.' Said I, 'What matter? For I will fend for us all, God helping me.' All she bought me was a shirt and some sheep's-hide shoes, and she gave me four reals and her blessing. And so one Tuesday, SEPTEMBER 7, 1595, at daybreak, I went forth from Madrid behind the trumpets of the Cardinal Prince.

We arrived that day at Alcalá de Henares and went to a church, where they held a great festival in honour of the Cardinal Prince. There was a man there selling marchpane, among many others, who had cards in his hands. And like a true little gamester, I untied my four reals from the tail of my shirt and began to play at all-fours. He won them of me, and my new shirt after them, and then the new shoes which I wore at my belt. I asked him if he would play me for my old hood. It was not long before I lost this too. So I was left with my naked body, a sign that I was to join the corps. And sure enough there were some who told me so, and even asked the sweetmeat-seller to give me a real; which he did, and a piece of marchpane for luck, by which methought I was the winner. That night I went off to the palace, and into the kitchen to enjoy the fire, for it was growing chilly. I slipped in with some other rascals, and on the morrow the trumpets sounded the departure for Guadalajara; so I had to follow for those four mortal leagues. With what was left of the real I bought some fritters, on which I marched all the way to Guadalajara. I begged the cook-boys to take pity on me, and let me mount awhile into the long cart in which they carried the kitchen-gear. They did not pity me, for they were not made that way.

We arrived at Guadalajara and I went off to the palace, for the kitchen fire had been grateful to me the night before. And without being told to, I had obliged them by helping to pluck the fowls and turn the spits, thanks to which I had supper that night. Now it seemed to Master Jaques, the chief cook of the Cardinal Prince, that I had borne myself civilly and obligingly, so he asked me from whence I came. I told him all, and how I was going to the wars. He ordered them to give me a good supper, and on the morrow to take me into the cart, which they did much against their will. I continued to work like the other scullions, making the best of myself, so that Master Jaques adopted me as his servant, and I came to be master of the kitchen, and of the long carts which went on ahead in the train of the Prince. Then did I avenge myself on certain of these rogues by making them go on foot for a day. But after this my anger was past.

We journeyed to Zaragoza, where there was much feasting, and from thence to Monsarrate and Barcelona; and I could take with me four or six persons without its costing me a farthing. Such are the results of good service. We lay at Barcelona a few days, until we set sail in twenty-six galleys, which had arrived from Genoa; and the Duke of Savoy entertained us much at Villefranche. From thence we passed to Savona. But before arriving we captured a ship, whether of the Turks or the Moors or the French I know not, but I believe we were then at war. It was good to me to see them fight with the artillery; and we took her.

We lay a few days at Savona, and then went off to Milan, where we stayed a few days; and from thence we took the road to Flanders through Burgundy, where we met many companies of horse and Spanish infantry, which made a strong squadron. I saw certain soldiers who, it seemed to me, were as much boys as I was, so I resolved to ask leave of my master, Master Jaques, who had taken a fancy to me. Not only did he refuse, but he told me that he would thrash me; upon which I was incensed, and drew up a memorial to His Highness, giving an account of everything, and how I had followed him from Madrid, and how his cook would not give me leave, for I wished to serve nobody but the King. He told me that I was a boy, but I answered that there were others in the companies; and on the morrow my memorial was returned with a decree, saying, 'Let him enlist, notwithstanding he is not of an age to serve.' Upon this my master was in despair; but as there was nothing to be done, he said that he could not do without me, and that until we arrived in Flanders I was to help him in every way he might need. I did so, serving more than ten soldiers, and the head of my squadron in particular. I enlisted in the company of Captain Mejía, but, after a few days' march, when we were drawing near to Flanders, the corporal of my squad, whom I respected even as the King, told me one night to follow him, for it was the captain's orders; and we left the army, for he had no love of fighting. When day broke we were far away, five leagues from the army. I said to him, 'Whither are we going?' He said, ' To Naples.' Upon which he loaded me with the haversack and took me to Naples, where I remained with him a few days, until I found myself in a ship which was going to Palermo.

Chapter ii

Of what happened up to my second return to Malta

⌒

I ARRIVED shortly (at Palermo), and was at once engaged as page and shield-bearer by Captain Felipe de Menargas, a Catalan. I served him with a will as page and shield-bearer, and he loved me well. He volunteered one day for the Levant, whither the galleys of Naples and Sicily were bound, with Don Pedro de Toledo as their Captain-General, and the galleys of Sicily under Don Pedro de Leyva. They were going to capture a land which is called Petrache (Patras). It fell to the lot of my captain's company to embark on the flagship of Cesar Latorre of the Sicilian squadron. We arrived at Patras, which is in the Morea, and landed our men, the squadron lying at anchor. The light or irregular troops attempted to scale the walls and make an entry. It was here that the first bullets whistled past my ears, for I stood before my captain with my shield and short lance. We took the place, but not the castle. There was much booty and many slaves, of which, though a boy, I got a good share, not on land, but on board the galley. For the soldiers, seeing that I was a person from whom it was not likely to be taken, gave me much stuff to look after. And as soon as we arrived in Sicily, I made myself a coat of many colours, out of what I had won. But a soldier from Madrid, who had given himself out to be a townsman of mine, and in whom I had trusted, wheedled out of me some clothes of the captain my master, saying that they were for play-acting. I thought he was telling the truth, and was to take me to the play; so I loaded him with all the clothes, which were very good – the best that my master had in his boxes, for he himself had chosen them – together with some buttons of gold and a hat-band. On the morrow the sergeant came to the house and told the captain that four soldiers had gone off; and one of them was my fellow-townsman. I was taken aback when I heard him, and, while appearing not to understand anything, I found out that the galleys of Malta were in port; and I went off and set sail in them. On arriving at Messina, I wrote a letter to the captain my master, giving him an account of my fellow-townsman's fraud, and how I had not asked leave of him out of fear. And so I made the voyage to Malta, and some Spanish gentlemen who were in the same galley undertook to place me in the service of the Grand Master's Receiver of Rents, an honourable knight named Gaspard de Monreal, who was very glad to have me serve him. I did so for a year to his great satisfaction, and at the end of that time I asked leave to go and be a soldier in Sicily; and the captain my master wrote a letter supporting my petition and saying how satisfied he was with me personally. Commander Monreal gave me leave, much to his regret, and sent me off with a fine suit.

I arrived at Messina, where the Viceroy, the Duke of Maqueda, was. I enlisted as a soldier in my captain's company, where I served as a soldier and not as a servant or page. A year later, the Viceroy fitted out a galliot to sail against the pirates, and ordered that the soldiers who desired to go in her should be given four days' pay in advance. I was one of them; and we sailed for Barbary. The captain was Ruy Pérez de Mercado. We met with nothing off the Barbary coast; but on our way back we fell in with another galliot a little smaller than our own at an island which they call Lampadosa (Lampedusa). We entered the bay, where they did not put up much of a fight, and we took her. On board of her we captured a corsair, the greatest of his day, named Caradali, and ninety more Turks with him. We were well received at Palermo by the Viceroy; and the recent capture whetted his appetite, for he armed two great galleons, one called the *Galleon of Gold* and the other the *Galleon of Silver*. I sailed in the *Galleon of Gold* and we left for the Levant, where we made so many captures that it would be too long to relate, and came back very rich, so that I, who was one of the soldiers at three crowns' pay a month, brought back more than three hundred crowns as my share in money and in kind. When we got back to Palermo, the Viceroy ordered that we should be given our shares of what had been brought home. There fell to my share a hat full to the brim with pieces of two, at which I began to be puffed up in spirit. But within a few days I had gambled it all away or spent it in other such riotous living.

He once more despatched the two galleons to the Levant, where we gained booty beyond belief, both by land and sea, so great was the luck of this Viceroy. We sacked the storehouses that were at Alexandretta, a seaport where they stored up in magazines all the merchandise brought overland

VAN DYCK: PHILIBERT, PRINCE OF ONEGLIA, VICEROY OF SICILY
(Dulwich Gallery)

from Portuguese India by Babylon and Aleppo. Great were the riches that we brought with us. During these voyages I scarcely slept; for I went mad on navigation, and was always instructing myself in the company of the pilots, watching them making charts, and getting to know about the lands which we passed, with their ports and capes, which I marked down. This afterwards served me for making a map of all the Levant, Morea and Anatolia and Caramania, Syria and Africa as far as Cape Cantin, which is on the [Atlantic] Ocean, and Cyprus and Sardinia, Mallorca and Minorca; the coast of Spain, from Cape St. Vincent, coasting along the shore, to Sanlúcar, Gibraltar, as far as Cartagena; and from thence to Barcelona and the coast of France as far as Marseilles; and from thence to Genoa; and from Genoa to Leghorn, the river Tiber and Naples; and from Naples the whole of Calabria till you get to Apulia and the Gulf of Venice, port by port, with its capes and creeks, and where all kinds of ships can be repaired, marking the depth of the water. This route-book is going the round here in my own hand, for Prince Philibert asked me if he could see it, and with him it remained.

We came to Palermo with all our riches; at which the Viceroy was very glad, and gave us such shares as he thought fit. With the freedom we enjoyed as the Viceroy's *Leventis* [which was the name given to the Turkish marines, who were wild and desperate men], and the money which he had, there was none who dared call us to account, for we went from inn to inn and from house to house.

One afternoon we went for our luncheon to an inn, as was our wont, and in the course of the meal one of my companions – for there were three of us – said, 'Bring us our food, you dirty dog!' The innkeeper said that he was no dog. On which my comrade drew his dagger and stabbed him in such wise that he never rose again.

The whole crowd fell upon us with spits and other weapons, so that we had need indeed to know how to defend ourselves. We went off to the church of Our Lady of the Grotto, where we remained in sanctuary till we saw how the Viceroy would take it. We heard that he had said he would be bound to hang us if he caught us. So, said I, 'Brothers, it is better to take cover than trust to the prayers of the saints.' So, putting together each his wretched mite, we made up a purse; and I had them bring us our arquebuses, without knowing why. They brought them, and since the church is by the sea-shore, and on the very harbour, I relied on my seamanship and cast my eyes on a felucca loaded with sugar. At midnight I said to my comrades, 'Now is the time. On board, worshipful sirs!' They said that people would hear us. Said I, 'There are none on board the felucca save the boy at the look-out.' So, boarding her, we gagged the boy and weighed anchor, telling him to be quiet or we would kill him. We took to the oars and began to row out of the creek; and as we passed the fort, they said, 'Boat ahoy!' We answered in Italian, 'Fishing boat,' on which they said no more. I turned the prow in the direction of Naples, which is three hundred miles across the sea; but, God being with us, we arrived without danger in three days. The harbour-master came to look at our papers. We told him the truth and how, in fear lest the Duke of Maqueda might hang us, we had fled as above related. The Viceroy was the Count of Lemos, the elder, and he had made his son captain of the infantry. This was Señor Don Francisco de Castro, who was afterwards Viceroy of Sicily, and is now

[27]

Count of Lemos, though he is a monk. The Count desired to look at us, and, seeing that we were personable, gallant fellows, he commanded that we should be enlisted in his son's company, and that the felucca should be sent to Palermo with the cargo of sugar which was in her. We were known in Naples as the Duke of Maqueda's *Leventis*, and they looked on us as godless men.

We spent a few days there in good repute, all three of us living as comrades in one house, and admitting no others. But one night there came to our house a soldier in the same company as ours, a Valencian, with one other. They gave themselves out to be gentlemen, and said to us, 'Be so good as to come with us, worshipful sirs; for a grievous thing has happened to us here in the Florentine quarter.' So, to keep up our reputation as *Leventis* we said, 'Let us go, in Christ's name!' And we left the goodwife alone in the house. Going along the road, we came upon a man who seemed to be making love. The Valencian hung behind, and we heard a cry. We went back to see what was the matter; and the Valencian came up with a hat and cloak, saying, 'That dog will howl no more!' 'Who was the fellow?' said I. 'A dog,' he said, 'whom I have sent to sup in hell, and who has left me this cloak.' I was scandalized to hear such words, and, coming up with one of my comrades, I said to him, 'God help us! We have come out to rob, and I am ill pleased with it.' He answered, 'Patience for this once, my friend. Let us not lose our reputation with these fellows.' 'I want no such reputation,' said I. We came to a house where they sold wine, which, as it seemed, was where they had been insulted. We entered by a back door and, words leading to blows, they began to beat the landlord, stabbing at the glass bottles, of which there were many, and likewise kicking about the wine-skins, so that they broke open and the wine flowed like a river. The landlord began to shout from the window, so we went out by the back door into the street. One of my comrades was struck down by a potsherd from the window, which bowled him right over, and he lay unconscious. So great was the shouting, that the Italian patrol came up, and we began to be hard pressed and to have our hands full. The fallen man could not get up, which worried me. At last we were so pressed by their muskets and their halberds that one of the Valencians had his wrist pierced by a halberd wound, and they captured him, together with the man who was lying on the ground. We retired towards our own quarters; but as the patrol were carrying off their prisoners, they stumbled upon the corpse from which the Valencian had taken the cloak. They reported it at the chief Spanish guard-room, and a patrol was at once sent out in search of my comrade and me and the other Valencian. We had taken leave of the Valencian and were on our way home, to fetch the wretched pittance which we had left there, and be off, when we saw the patrol with lighted torches at our door. 'Friend,' said I, 'every man for himself, since you would not listen to me about the cloak.' And, dashing down an alley, I made for the jetty, and knocked at an inn which is there beside the Custom House, where there was a Knight of the Order of St. John, who had come from Malta to fit out a galleon for the Levant, a friend of mine called Captain Betrian. When he saw me, he was startled. I told him the truth; and he hid me and kept me for twenty days, until he was about to sail. And that night he got me on board, and put me in the place where they store the biscuit, where I sweated my fill till we were outside Naples; when he fetched me out and carried me with a good will to Malta. But the Valencian and my comrade whom they knocked down with a flower-pot were hanged within ten days. Of my other comrades I never heard again.

Chapter iii

Of what happened up to the Miracle of the Isle of Lampedusa

ᔕ

A T Malta Commander Monreal was glad to see me; and, after spending a few days there, we sailed for the Levant with a galleon and a frigate. We were more than two months without capturing a prize. But one day, as we were about to put into port at Cape Silidonia (Chelidonia), we found inside a saucy Moorish caramuzal, which was like a galleon. We attacked it, and the Turks flung themselves into the boats and made for land to save their freedom. The captain ordered us to go after them, offering ten crowns for every slave. There was a big pine-wood there, and I was one of the soldiers who leapt on land in pursuit of the Turks. I carried my sword and a shield, but no trace of a beard had I. I lay in ambush in the pine-wood, where I came upon a Turk like a regular Goliath, who was shouting to the others, and bore in his hand a pike, from which flew a flag of orange and white. I went straight up to him and said, 'Down with you!' But the Turk looked on me and laughed, saying some words in Turkish which I knew to be a foul insult. I was furious. I gripped my shield and went straight for him. And so, getting in under the point of his pike, I gave a thrust at his breast which felled him to the ground.

I took the flag from the pike and girt it round me. And I was stripping him, when two French soldiers came up, saying, 'Halves!' I rose from stooping over the Turk and, gripping my buckler, I told them to leave him alone, for he was mine, and if they did not I would kill them. They thought this a great joke, and we began to lay on to one another in style, when four other soldiers came up with three Turks whom they had captured, and made peace between us. On this we all went off together to the galleon, taking no spoils from the wounded man. The captain was told all about it, and when he had heard the Turk's statement, he said that I alone was the owner of all. The Frenchmen almost mutinied, for I was the only Spaniard in all that galleon, and there were more than a hundred Frenchmen. So the captain had to leave things as they were till we came to Malta and laid it before the Lords of the Tribunal of Armament. The Turk carried more

than 400 gold sequins; the caramuzal had a cargo
of soap from Cyprus. We put a crew on board her
and sent her to Malta; and we stayed behind to seek
more prizes. We went out to meet the cruisers of
Alexandria; and towards nightfall we sighted a
ship, a very great one to all appearance, as indeed
she was. We followed in her wake so as not to lose
her, and so we encountered her at midnight. And
having turned our artillery on her, we asked,
'What ship are you?' 'A sea-going ship,' was the
answer. She too had made ready, and thought
nothing of a single ship, for she carried more than
four hundred Turks, and was well equipped with
artillery. So she gave us a single broadside which
alone carried off seventeen of our men to the other
world, not to speak of the wounded. We let her
have one back, giving as good as we got. They
boarded us, and there was a stiff fight, for they had
managed to gain our forecastle, and it was tough
work forcing them back on to their own ship. And
thus we remained all night until the next day. At
daybreak we went after her and she did not run
away. But our captain made use of a stratagem
which stood us in good stead, for he left on deck no
more men than were necessary, and closed down all

the hatches, so that we had to fight or jump into the sea. It was a stiff engagement, for we gained possession of their forecastle for a good long time, till they turned us out of it; upon which we sheered off and fought with our artillery, for we were better sailors and stronger in guns. And here I saw two miracles that day, to which I have witnesses; and this is how it was: a Dutch gunner exposed himself while loading a gun, and they shot at him with another and hit him on the middle of the head, blowing it to smithereens and bedewing with his brains all those around him. And a bone from his head struck a sailor on the nose, which had been crooked from his birth; but when he was cured, his nose remained as straight as mine, only with a scar from the wound. There was another soldier, a mass of aches and pains, who would let nobody sleep in his mess with his calling on the saints and blaspheming; but that day he was shot at by a cannon, and the ball shaved his two buttocks. And never more, during the whole voyage, did he complain of his aches; so that he used to say that he had never sweated better than in the draught from a cannon-ball. We continued our fight that day on the high seas, and, as night came on, the enemy tried to make an effort and run aground, for the land was near. We followed them, and at daybreak we all found ourselves becalmed quite near the land. It was the day of Our Lady of the Conception; and the captain gave orders that all the wounded should come up on deck to die, for, said he, 'Gentlemen, either we sup with Christ or at Constantinople.' Up they all came, and I with them; for I had a thigh pierced through with a musket shot, and a great wound in the head which I had got from a partisan the day before as I was boarding the enemy's ship, when we captured their forecastle. We had with us as our chaplain a monk, a Calced Carmelite, and the captain said to him, 'Father, give us a blessing, for it is our last day.' The good monk did so, and when he had finished, the captain ordered the frigate to tow us up to the other ship, which was very near. We drew alongside, and so great was the battle between us that however much we might have wished to get away from them, it was impossible; for they had thrown over us from the other ship a big anchor with a great chain lest we might cast loose. It lasted more than three hours, and at the end of this time it was recognized that victory was ours. For the Turks, seeing that they were near the land, began throwing

themselves into the sea, not noticing that our frigate
was going round fishing them out. Our victory
was complete. So, after securing the slaves, we gave
ourselves over to sacking the ship; and the booty
was rich and great. There were so many dead that
there were more than two hundred and fifty below,
whom they had not wished to throw into the sea
lest we might see them. We threw them overboard.
And I saw that day a thing by which you may know
what manner of men Christians are; for among the
numbers of dead whom we threw into the sea, there
was one who remained face uppermost, unlike the
Moors and Turks, who, when you throw their
corpses into the sea, at once turn face and body
downwards, but the Christians turn them upwards.
We asked the Turks whom we had taken prisoner
how it was that this man remained face uppermost,
and they said they had always suspected him of
being a Christian, and that he was a baptized renegade, and at the time when he abjured his faith he
was a man of French nationality. We repaired our
ship and the prize – and they both needed it – and
we set our course for Malta, where we arrived shortly
after. And since the prize was so rich, the captain
ordered that no one should gamble, so that every

man should come rich to Malta. He gave orders to
throw dice and cards into the sea, and laid a heavy
penalty on any one who should play. And so they
arranged a game, in the following manner: they
made a circle on a table as big as the palm of one's
hand, and in the middle of it, another circle as small
as a piece of eight, and into this little circle each
player put a louse. Each man kept an eye on his
own, and they laid very heavy wagers on them.
The first louse to leave the big circle took all the
stakes, and I vow they ran as high as eighty sequins.
When the captain saw how determined we were,
he allowed any man to play who would. So great
is the vice of gambling in the soldier!

At Malta I brought a lawsuit about my slave
whom I captured on land at Cape Silidonia. And
when I had done what was necessary in every
quarter, the Lords of Armament gave judgment
that the four hundred sequins should be counted as
part of the prize-money, and that a bounty of a
hundred ducats should be given me for the prisoner
and the flag, with the privilege of bearing it on my
arms as a trophy if I wished; which I did with much
content, and bestowed the flag upon the church of
Our Lady of Grace. What with my prize-money

and the booty, there fell to my share more than fifteen hundred ducats, which I squandered in a short time. So, seeing that the galleys of the Order were about to sail for the Levant to perform some exploit, I set sail with them as an adventurer; and in twenty-four days we were there and back, having taken a fortress which is in the Morea, which is called Pasaba, from which they carried off five hundred persons – what with men and women and children – the Governor with his wife, children, and horses, and thirty pieces of artillery cast in bronze; and all this – to the surprise of everybody – without losing a man. It is true that they thought we were the Christian fleet which had gathered together at Messina. Later on in the same year, which was 1601, the same galleys went off to Barbary to perform another exploit. I sailed as an adventurer, as on the last voyage, and we went and took a city called La Mahometa (Hammamet); and this was how it happened: We came in sight of land the night before we performed this exploit, and we made very little way until morning, for we were very near. The Captain-General gave orders that we were all to put turbans on our heads and lower the fore-yard, so that we seemed to be the galliots of Morato

Rais; and such they thought us to be, with our flags flying, and our Turkish pennons, and playing on kettle-drums and shawms in the Turkish manner. In this wise we managed to cast anchor very near in shore. The inhabitants of the city, which is on the very edge of the water, came out almost to a man — children, women and men. Three hundred men had been told off for this exploit, and they were not slothful in carrying it out. They soon rushed the gates and took them, with which the capture was complete. I was one of the three hundred. We collected together all the women and children, and a few men, for many of them fled. We entered in and sacked the place, but the booty was poor, for they are miserable nomads. We took on board seven hundred souls and our wretched spoils. But there soon came up more than three thousand Moors, both foot and horse, to relieve them, on which we set fire to the town and sailed away. It cost us three gentlemen and five soldiers, who were ruined by their covetousness. So that we returned to Malta with contentment, and I squandered the trifle that I had won. For the wenches of that land are so fair and so wily that they are mistresses of all that belong to both gentlemen and soldiers.

CARAVAGGIO: ALOF DE VIGNACOURT, GRAND MASTER OF THE ORDER OF
ST. JOHN OF JERUSALEM

(Louvre)

DE CONTRERAS

A few days after this the Grand Master, the Lord Vinancour (Vignacourt), ordered me to the Levant with a frigate, to gather information about the movements of the Turkish warships, by reason of the experience which I had of the country and the language. What with oarsmen and other soldiers, the frigate carried thirty-seven persons, of whom I was captain; and they gave me my commission signed and sealed by the Grand Master. I went and entered the Archipelago. I got news from certain ships of how the fleet had passed out from between the forts and was lying at an island called Tenedos, from whence it would shape its course for Chios.

I hung about till I saw that it had arrived at Chios; and when I knew it was there, I looked out to see whether it would go to Negropont, which is in the Morea, outside the Archipelago. For, unless I could find out for certain whether it was going to Christian lands or staying in its own waters, I should have done nothing. Now you must know that every year the General of the Seas goes forth from Constantinople to visit the Archipelago; for many of the islands are inhabited by Greeks, but the governors are Turks. On his voyage he collects the tribute, which forms his revenue, and dispenses justice, and inflicts and remits punishment; besides which all the islands keep a present for him, each according to its resources, and he has royal rights and appoints the governors. He takes with him the Royal Galley, with twenty more that are stationed at Constantinople; the squadron of Rhodes, which numbers nine; the two from Cyprus and one of the two from Alexandria; two from Tripoli in Syria; one from Egypt; another from Nápoles (Nauplia) in Romania; three from Chios; another two from Negropont; another from the Caballa squadron; another from Mytilene. These do not belong to the Grand Turk, but only those of Constantinople and Rhodes, for the rest belong to the governors who govern the lands which I have mentioned. I had forgotten the two from Damietta, which is at the outlet of the Nile; there are two galleys there, and they make their visit together, as I have said, to the Archipelago. But when they are to go forth from the Archipelago, and go to Christian territories, they are joined by those of Barbary, Algiers, Bizerta, Tripoli, and others, which arm themselves to form part of the fleet, as they did this year. But if they do not come to Negropont to clean the hulls and take in supplies, it cannot be concluded that they are going to Christian lands. I knew for sure that they were careening and shipping stores at Negropont, and I went to wait at Cape Mayna. And from the said cape I descried the fleet, which was of fifty-three galleys with a few brigantines. I left for the island of Sapienza, which is over against Modon, a fortified town of the Turks near Navarino. From thence I came to Zante, a city of the Venetians, on a fertile island, and I stayed there till I knew it had started from Navarino. Then I crossed to Chifalonia (Cefalonia), also an island of the Venetians, and from thence I came by sea to Calabria, which is a distance of four hundred miles. I landed on the first shore I came to, and gave warning that the fleet was coming; and, coasting round the shore, I continued to give warning till I arrived at Ríjoles (Reggio), which I had had sure information that the enemy was going to sack, as another general, his predecessor, had done, who was called Cigala. I was well received by the Governor of Ríjoles, who was a Knight of the Military Order of St. John, named Rotinel; and he made ready, summoning the men of his district and the gentry. And it was necessary to make good haste, for the fleet had cast anchor in the Fossa di San Giovanni, fifteen miles distant from Ríjoles. On the third day, we knew, by the horsemen who came and went between the Fossa di San Giovanni and Ríjoles, that they were landing men from the fleet. The Governor laid an ambush for them, which wiped out three hundred Turks and took sixty prisoners; on which they returned on board without doing any harm. As for me, the Governor ordered me to set sail in my frigate and cross the Fossa and give warning to the cities of Tabormina (Taormina) and Caragoça (Syracuse) and Agusta (Agosta), which are on the coast of Sicily opposite San Giovanni, at a distance of twenty miles. Which I did, crossing through the midst of the enemy's fleet. And, having done as he commanded me, I passed over to Malta, and gave warning of all I have related. They took careful measures, so that when the fleet came to the island of Gozo, where we have good fortifications, they were already on their guard. And when the enemy wished to land, the knights who are in this island would not allow them, nor would they let them take water on board. Such was the end of the Turkish fleet in our territories this year. We passed a few days with the wenches, and then I was sent to Barbary to reconnoitre El Cantara, which is a fortress of Barbary near by Gelves (Djerba), from whence oil is shipped. And there were lying two hookers newly laden with oil for the Levant. I went forth from the port of Malta with my frigate well armed, shaping my course towards Barbary. Halfway there is an island which is called Lampadosa, where we captured Caradali, the corsair. It has a harbour large enough for six galleys, and there is a tower commanding the port, of great size, but deserted. They say it is enchanted, and that it was in this island that King Roger gave battle to Bradamante – a fable, to my mind. But it is no fable that there is a cavern there which is entered on the level. In it there is an image of Our Lady, with the Babe in her arms, painted on canvas upon a very ancient slab of wood, which works many miracles. In this cave is her altar, on which is the image, with many things left there as offerings by the Christians, including biscuit, cheese, oil, bacon, wine, and money. On the other side of the cave is a tomb in which, they say, is buried a Turkish marabout, who, they say, is a saint of theirs, and receives the same offerings as our image, more or less, and much Turkish clothing; only he has no bacon. And sure it is that these offerings of food are left by both Christians

D

and Turks, so that when any runaway slave arrives
there, he may have wherewithal to feed himself till
a vessel of his nation arrives and takes him away,
be he Christian or Turk. We have seen this; for
when we were with the galleys of the Order, some
Moors ran away from us, and, after hiding here until
a Moorish ship arrived, they embarked upon her. In
the meantime, they ate of these victuals. It is in this
wise that those who lie hidden here find out whether
the ships belong to the Christians or the Moors: the
island has a tower, as aforesaid, on which they
mount, keeping a look-out to seaward; and when a
ship comes in, they go by night among the bushes
down to the port. By the language which is spoken,
it is easy to recognize whether it is their own nation.
They hail them and embark; and this happens every
day. But be it noted that neither that ship nor any
other will dare to take so much as the value of a pin
out of the cave; for, if she did, it would be impossible for her to get out of the port. And this
we have seen every day. The lamp of the Virgin
is wont to remain burning by night and by day,
with never a soul on the island. The same island
so abounds in land-turtles that we load up our galleys when we go thither; and there are many coneys.

It is as flat as your hand; its coasts measure eight miles round.

All these offerings, which are many, the image will allow no ship of any nation to take away, except the galleys of Malta, and they take them to the Church of the Annunziata at Trapani. If anyone else takes them, he cannot get outside the port.

Chapter iv

In which are continued my Voyages in the Levant
and what came to pass until I came to the
Island of Estampalia

～

I SAILED on my way that night, shaping my course
towards Barbary, and found myself at daybreak
on the bank, which is ten miles long. On it there was
lying a galliot of seventeen benches, which I was
ill pleased to see. The same, when she sighted me,
ran up a green standard with three crescents, which
streamed down to the water. My men began to be
dismayed, and the ship's master said, 'Woe is me!
Now are we slaves, for it is the galliot of Said Mami
of Tripoli.' I gave him the lie, saying, 'Come, boys,
to-day we shall make a fine prize.' I stopped in my
course and ceased sailing, that I might put myself
in a state of defence. I set my small culverin in
order, and filled her up with nails and bullets and
little bags of stones, saying: 'Leave it to me and the
galliot is ours. Let each man take his sword in hand
and his shield at his side, and the soldiers stand by
with muskets' (for I had eight who were Spaniards

and whom I could trust). I began to draw near to the galliot. She lay still. And she did right, for I durst not flee, though some were minded to do so; for it would have been blank ruin, not to speak of the shame. 'Friends,' said I to them, 'do you not see that between us and any Christian land there are a hundred and twenty miles; while that ship has a full crew, and in four strokes of the oars will have the grappling anchor on us? And if we flee, we prove them the better men? Leave it to me to act, for I too have a life. Look now, when we draw alongside we will sail past her and give her the full charge of our musketry. They will throw themselves down flat to receive it; and when they get up to return our fire, I will let fly at them with the culverin, which I have loaded, and wipe them out.' This seemed good to them. So, running up our flags, I advanced to the attack with a high courage, at which they stood amazed. Seeing that I was resolute, as soon as we drew near the galliot, she took flight. I followed her for more than four hours, without managing to overtake her, and I gave orders that they should cease rowing and that the men should eat. The galliot did likewise, without drawing away from us. I resumed the chase and she her flight, till evening came, when I did the same thing. I lay quiet all the evening and the night, keeping good watch lest she might go off under cover of darkness, and I continue my voyage to La Cantara. Before daybreak I gave the men breakfast and wine without water, in view of what might turn up; and when day had broken I found the galliot within arquebus shot. I turned my prow towards her and began to overtake her, firing on her with the muskets. They rowed hard to escape me. I followed in like manner. And I would not leave them till I had forced them to run aground below the fortress of Gelves, where they jumped on shore with water up to their waists, for all that part is shallow. And, although they fired off a few pieces, that did not stop me from throwing a cable on to the galliot and towing her outside, out of range of the artillery. Two Christians, who were slaves, had stayed on board her, one a Majorcan and the other a Sicilian from Trapani. There were a few trifles such as muskets, and bows and arrows, and a little clothing. I took off her sails and flag; but as for the boat, I gave orders to burn it, with a lot of trash which I did not want, for fear of over-loading the frigate. I set off from thence, shaping my course for La Cantara, but not a boat was there at the magazines. I forgot to say from whence the galliot came: she was from Santa Maura, and was on her way to Barbary to be fitted out for piracy.

From La Cantara I betook myself to Old Tripoli, and in a creek twelve miles away I lay with my masts taken down for the whole of a day and a night. On the morrow at daybreak there passed by a *garbo* laden with jars and carrying seventeen Moors, both men and women. Not one of them escaped me. I took them on to my frigate and sank the boat, from which I took off a jar full of saffron, and a few pieces of waterproof woollen stuff. I shaped my course for Malta, where I was well received. They gave me my share of the money for the slaves, who are bought by the Order at sixty crowns each, taking the good with the bad; and of the residue my share came to seven per cent. I squandered it lightheartedly with my friends and the wench, for it was she who had the lion's share of all that I won with such toil. At this time there came round the feast of St. Gregory, which is held six miles outside the city. All the people go thither, together with the Grand Master, and not a wench is left in the town. I ought to have gone, but, on account of the jealousy I felt, I would not go myself nor let my wench go either. That day, after dinner, I was with the said wench, discoursing of our mutual jealousy, when I heard a gun fired on the Castle of St. Elmo – which was a strange thing – and close upon it another. I sallied forth into the street, where men were shouting that the slaves were escaping from the bakeries of the Order, where they make the bread for all belonging to it. I set out at once for Borgo, where I had my frigate, and thought I should find my men; but I was at a loss what to do, for they had gone to San Gregorio. So I took some of the watermen, who earn their living by ferrying people across the water, and I manned the frigate, taking in her nothing but the culverin and some short pikes. I went forth from the port in pursuit of the slaves, who were going off in a good boat, hoisting a sheet as a flag. As I drew near I called upon them to surrender; but they, like their impudence, said I might come and fetch them. There were twenty-three of them, and they carried three bows with a quantity of arrows, and two cutlasses and more than thirty spits. I once again called upon them to beware, for I was sure to sink them. Let them surrender, I said, and I should do them no harm, for they were bound to seek their freedom. They would not surrender, saying that they would rather die, since they had lost their liberty. I fired off the culverin and broke the legs of four of them. And as I drew alongside, they let fly a discharge of arrows, which killed one of my sailors and wounded two. I boarded them, and, having tied their hands together, I put them in the frigate and the boat which I towed after me. It so happened that I had disabled one of them, who was their leader, and he lay dying of his wounds. But before he had done with it I strung him up by one foot, and, hoisting him aloft, I entered the harbour, where all the inhabitants of the city were upon the walls, with the Grand Master, who had come up when he heard the firing. They had carried off more than twelve thousand ducats worth of silver and jewels of their masters', for, although they were escaping from the bakery, not more than four of them belonged to it; but the others belonged to private persons. I knew the value of what I had done, and made the most of it. I jumped ashore and kissed the Grand Master's hand. And he thought highly of my service, and ordered that I should be given two hundred crowns. But had I not helped myself, I should not have touched a real, for those gentlemen who were the slaves' masters – counsellors every one of them – held me responsible, and one of them even sued me for payment on account of the one I had hanged. Nothing came of it, and hanged he remained. And my wench was glad that she had not gone to the feast; for she enjoyed all that I stole from the boat, out of which she has at this very day a mighty fine house, built at my expense.

A few days later it came to pass that three Capuchin fathers were on their way to Malta. They had embarked in a boat laden with wood; but a brigantine came out and captured them. The Grand Master heard of it, and at midnight he sent for me and ordered me at all costs to set out from port in search of the brigantine, even if I had to go as far as Barbary. I did so, and, having come to Sicily, to the tower of Pozal (Pozzallo), I got information that the brigantine was on its way to Licata. I followed her, and was there told that she had gone to Surjento (Girgenti); and there I was told that she had gone to Marçara (Mazzara); and there they told me that she had gone to Maritimo, an island on the way to Barbary, where there is a small fort of the King's. They said that she had set out from thence for Barbary seven hours ago. I resolved to follow her. The men mutinied against me, because I was not carrying the necessary victuals, which was the truth. But I was counting upon finding on our way the Mother of God at Lampadosa, from whom, and from the marabout, we should have taken all our victuals, with the intention of paying for them; and so I said to them all, upon which they were appeased. I set sail, in the name of God, shaping my course for Barbary, and in less than eight hours the look-out descried the boat from aloft. I forged ahead, both by oar and sail, lest the daylight should fail me, and overhauled her inch by inch. The brigantine resolved to put in at an island called Calinosa (Linosa), thinking that she would escape; for night was falling. But I made such good haste that I forced her to run ashore on the island before she had intended. All the Moors fled, being seventeen in number, and I found the brigantine with none but the three monks and a woman and a boy aged fourteen, and an old man. I refloated her and left her under a good guard till morning. It was pitiful to see the Fathers with the manacles on their hands. We had supper; and in the morning I sent two careful men to the highest point of the island to keep a look-out towards the sea, and one was to stay there on the look-out and the other to come down with whatever news they might have. He said that the sea was clear of boats; on which I sent him to the wood, which was a tiny one, to set fire to it on four sides; when all the seventeen Moors came out into the open, not one of them being missing. I took them all prisoner, and put half of them into the frigate and the other half into the brigantine, with half my own men; and in this wise we set sail, shaping our course for Malta, where you can imagine with what joy we entered. The voyage was worth three hundred gold pieces of twenty reals to me, besides my gratuity, with which my wench regaled herself.

A few days later they sent me to the Levant to collect information. I made all ready and started from Golfo Lançado. The first land at which I touched was Zante, at a distance of six hundred miles from Malta, half-way to the Archipelago, and at the island of Cerfanto (Sifanto) I came one morning upon a small dismasted brigantine manned by ten Greeks. I put them on board my frigate, and asked them whither they were going in this

plight. They said, 'To Chios.' But, being an artful
fellow, I asked them where they kept the Turks
whom they had on board. They denied with oaths
that there were any. 'But what about these *tapa-
cines?*' said I. 'Whose are they? Do you not see
that they are what the Turks eat from? And you
say you have none on board?' They denied it. I
began to put them to the torture, and not in play
either. They all stood it except a boy of fifteen,
whom I had stripped and bound and set upon a
low stone. 'Tell me the truth,' I said. 'If not, I
will cut off your head with this knife.' When he
saw that I meant it, the father of the boy came and
threw himself at my feet, and said to me, 'Ah, captain, do not kill my son, for I will tell you where
the Turks are.' And this very man had befouled
himself under the torment. See what the love of
children can do! Some soldiers went off and fetched
three Turks, one gentleman and his two men-
servants, with his robe of scarlet furred with marten,
and his damascened knives, with their slender
silver chain. He threw himself at my feet, with his
well-trimmed red beard and all. I sent the brigantine off with the Greeks. But I was forgetting that
they brought with the Turks five chests – those

Turkish ones with rounded tops – full of damask of different colours, and much crimson floss silk, and a few pairs of little baby shoes.

I tried to get information and he gave me some, for he was on his way from Constantinople with a laden caramuzal; but for fear of the corsairs he was travelling by that small brigantine, which seemed to him to be safe; and this was reasonable. He told me how the Turkish fleet was on its way to the Black Sea; so that my mind was made easy, and I asked him whether he wished to be ransomed. He said, 'Yes.' We came to an understanding, after long bargaining, that he would give me three thousand gold sequins; but for this purpose he had to pledge the credit of two sons in Athens, from whence he came. I went thither, but would not enter the harbour, for it has a narrow mouth, and with twenty arquebusiers they can, if they will, keep you from coming out. I went to a creek which is five miles from this place. It was necessary to despatch one of the two servants, giving him three hours and no more to get there and back. This he did, and with him returned all the nobility of Athens on horseback. When I saw such a band of horsemen, I put out to sea; but they hoisted a

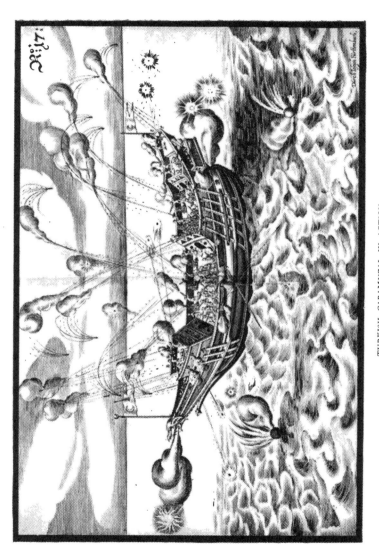

TURKISH CARAMUZAL IN ACTION

(From J. Fürttenbach, *Architectura navalis*, 1629)

white towel on a pike, upon which I was reassured, and ran up the ensign of St. John. Three venerable Turks came on board, and I must needs go ashore and come to terms. I treated with one who, it seemed, must have been the Governor, from their respectful bearing towards him. He told me they could not raise the money till the next day. I answered that I would be off and have done with it; for he knew quite well that it was not far by land to Negropont, and they might send warning to Morato Gancho, who was the pasha of that town; and he might come with his galley of twenty-six benches and capture me. But if the Governor were prepared to give me surety both by sea and land, I would wait till such time as he might appoint. He told me that he could not by sea, but that he would by land. 'Then give me leave,' said I, 'for I am off; and you can whistle for your Turks who are on board the frigate.' When he saw that I was resolute, he said he was well pleased to do as aforesaid; and so, before them all, he raised his finger, saying *Lala il Allah*, by which an oath is made more binding than twenty written guarantees. We spoke of many things, for he understood Spanish. It may be noted that he had already sent to summon Morato Gancho.

We ate of a heifer which they had slaughtered, and instead of wine we drank of a cordial made from raisins of Corinth. They wanted me to get on a horse. I said that I had no skill in riding aught but the sea. They themselves mounted and galloped and skirmished, which was a sight to see, for their horses were fine, and all wore about their haunches short coverings of damask of varied hues; and there were more than two hundred and fifty of them. They brought the money in pieces of eight, freshly minted at Segovia, and asked me to accept these, as they had no gold. I told the ship's master to take and count them, but it seemed to him that with so much new money, so far from where it was minted, there might be some trick. He came to me and told me this. I ordered him to cut one of them, and the core of it was of copper and the outside of silver. I protested at once, but they swore by Allah that they were no party to it, and were ready to kill the two Venetian merchants who had brought the money; and they would have done so had I not intervened. They begged me to have patience, while they returned to the city to fetch the money; and four Turks on four horses were off like the wind. While we were in this plight, the galliot of Morato

Gancho hove in sight at the mouth of the creek. When I saw her I turned cold all over; and the Athenians at once got on horseback and hoisted a white flag on the end of a lance. The galley steered towards them, and they made her drop anchor about the distance of an arquebus shot from me; for such is the faith of a Turk! And when the captain had landed, he came up to where I was standing with some other Turks. I advanced to meet him, and we saluted each other, he according to his usages and I according to mine. He went and saw him whom I had captured as my slave, first asking my leave. I at once ordered that the captive should be brought on shore, with his robe and his knives, just as I captured him; which they esteemed a great favour. We conversed agreeably, and they asked me to go and see the galley. We went, and on my entry I was saluted with shawms. I stayed there a while, and then we went on shore, and passed the time in conversation till the messengers came with the money, and they were not so much as two hours going and coming. They brought it me in sequins of gold; and over and above this, they presented me with two cotton cloths like silk, two silver-mounted cutlasses, two bows and two quivers, with five hun-

dred arrows glittering with gold, much bread and
spirits, and two heifers. I gave orders to fetch the
floss silk and the babies' shoes and gave them to him
who was my captive, who kissed me in return for
this. Moreover, I gave him a piece of damask, and
presented another to the master of the galley, and
he gave me some knives with damascened blades.
By this time it was nightfall; but when I sought to
depart, he asked me to sup with him and leave in
the morning. I accepted, and he feasted me well.
While we were at supper, my captive sent a note to
the master, begging to ransom his two servants, first
asking my permission. He besought me so earnestly
that I at once sent for them to the frigate, and said
to him, 'Behold, they await your pleasure.' He
esteemed this a great favour. He would have given
me two hundred sequins. I would not accept them;
so he said to me, 'Take then this Christian who is my
servant here in the poop.' I told him I would accept,
for so the man would recover his freedom. I departed
to my frigate, and in the morning I sent to ask his
leave to weigh anchor. He replied, whenever I
liked. I did so; and as I passed near by the galley I
gave him a salute from my culverin. He returned
it with another piece, upon which each of us went

his own way. I shaped my course towards the channel of Rhodes and arrived at an island called Estampalia (Stampalia) with a large settlement of Greeks. There is no civil governor there, but a Greek with a commission from the General of the Seas acts as military governor. I was well known and esteemed in all these islands, for I had never done them harm, rather I had aided them whensoever I might. When I captured any prize from the Turks, and could not take it to Malta, I gave them the boat out of charity, and sold them the grain or rice and flax, which were the cargoes they generally carried. So much was this the case, that when there was any great dispute, they would say, 'Let us wait for Captain Alonso' – for so they called me – 'that he may give judgment.' And when I came they would tell me all, and I would give judgment, even if they had to wait a year. And my word was law, as if it had been the word of a Royal Council. And afterwards we all supped together, both parties alike.

Chapter v

Which continues till the Time when I came to Malta again from the Levant

◡

ARRIVED at Estampalia, I entered the harbour. It was a feast-day; and so soon as they knew that it was I, they took counsel together, and at once there came out almost all the people, with Captain George (for that was the governor's name), calling upon me as *O morfo pulicarto*, which means, 'Young gallant.' There came many married women and maidens, in bodices with skirts falling to the knees, and coloured jackets, having the upper half of the sleeve almost tight to the arm, but flaring out in a rounded cuff half across the body. They wore coloured stockings and shoes, and some of them had pattens open at the toe. Some wear them of velvet the same colour as their dress; those who can of silk, and those who cannot of scarlet. Their beads, which among us are worn round the throat, are worn here round the brow; and whoso can wears ear-rings and bracelets of gold on her wrists. Among them were many of my gossips, whose children I had held at the font. They all came sad and weeping, and begging me with much clamour to be their judge; for a frigate of the Christians had carried off by guile their *papaz* – that is, their priest – and had asked for him two thousand sequins. I asked where he was, and when he had been captured. They said, that very morning, and they had not heard mass, and the hour was then two in the afternoon. Again I questioned them, 'Where, then, is the frigate of the Christians which took him away?' They said, 'At the Careenage,' which is an island about two miles away. I turned my frigate thitherwards; and this was quite in order, for I was bound to fight them, Christians though they might be: since they are men who take up arms without a licence, evil-livers all; and they rob both Moors and Christians, as has been seen, since they captured the priest and held him to ransom for two thousand sequins. To cut a long story short, I arrived at the islet with arms in hand and artillery in readiness. I found the frigate flying a flag with the image of Our Lady. She was a little frigate, with nine benches, and a crew of twenty. I at once ordered her captain on board my frigate. He obeyed on the spot, and I asked him where he had fitted his ship. He said, 'At Messina.' I asked him for his commission, and he gave it me; but it was a forged one. Upon this I made half the crew come on board my frigate, and had them put in irons, and I sent a like number on to his frigate. They began to protest, saying that it was not their fault; that Jacomo Panaro – for such was their captain's name – had deceived them saying that he had a commission from the Viceroy; and that they would go to the end of the world to serve me, but they would not go an inch for the other; that they had not known he intended to capture the priest; and as soon as they had seen my frigate enter the harbour, the captain had wanted to flee with the priest; but they would not do so, and had waited. For these reasons I decided that I would not put them in irons; but I set the captain on shore on the island, naked and with no provisions, so that he should pay for his sin there by dying of hunger. I went off with the two frigates; and when I arrived at the harbour, nearly all the people were gathered together there. I set the priest ashore, and as soon as they saw him they began to cry aloud and bless me a thousand times. They heard how I had left the captain on the island, naked and with no food, and begged me on their knees to send for him. I

told them not to bother me, for that was the way
to punish robbers and enemies of the Christians;
let them be thankful I had not hanged him. We
went up to the church of that place, leaving the
frigates under guard, and nobody came up with me
save one of my comrades. When we entered the
church, those of them who were most like gentlemen, if there be any such in those parts – I mean
the most distinguished of them, for in every place
there are some more so and some less – sat down on
the benches. They placed me by myself in a chair,
with a carpet under my feet, and after a while the
priest came forth, vested as for a feast-day, and
began to chant, and the people all responded with
Cristo saneste, which is their way of giving thanks
to God. He censed me, and then kissed me on the
cheek; and afterwards came all the people, first the
men and then the women, and did the same; and
sure it is that there were some right comely women,
whose kisses grieved me not at all, for they were some
antidote to all those given me by so many bearded
men – and great beards they had, too. We came out
from thence and went to the captain's house, where
the priest and the family stayed to dinner; and they
sent at once to the frigates much wine and bread

and cooked meat and fruit, of which they had an abundance.

We sat down to dinner, which was plenteous and good. They seated me at the head of the table. I would not consent, but bade them seat the priest there. There sat down with us the captain's wives and his daughter, who was a virgin both lovely and well attired. We ate, and many healths were drunk; and when the meal was over, I said that I must be gone to the frigate. The priest arose with much solemnity and said, 'Captain Alonso, the men and women of this place have shut the gates on you; and they beg and pray you to be their chief and protector, by taking in marriage this the lady daughter of Captain George, who will give you all his possessions, and we ours. And we will go surety for it that the General of the Seas shall give you the position of captain, for what with a present that we shall make him, and paying him the accustomed haratch (tax paid by non-Moslems), there will be no objection, and all of us will become your obedient slaves. And take note that we have sworn this in the church, and that it cannot be otherwise. In God's name, grant us this desire which we have had for many days.' I replied that it was not possible for me to do as they desired, for I must return to Malta and render an account of the mission entrusted to me. Besides which, it would bring reproach upon my name; for it would be said that I had not remained behind to marry in a Christian land and with a Christian, but in Turkey, denying the faith which I hold so high. Moreover, the men whom I had brought with me were in the very heart of Turkey and might come to grief; and if so, then I should be the cause of their ruin, and of the loss of their freedom. But, although they judged my reasons to be of weight, so great was the desire that possessed them, that they told me I must stay there. Seeing how firm was their resolve, I said that my comrade must go to the frigates and make trial to see how my men would take it; and according to what he saw, I would act.

My comrade went down and related what had happened, at which they all marvelled. But if they loved me up yonder, how much more did my men! So that they began to arm themselves, and took a culverin out of each of the frigates and mounted them on top of a windmill which stood before the town gates a little distance off. And they sent back word by my comrade that if I were not let out, they would force an entrance and sack the place; and that this was the best recompense they could make for all the good I had always done them. The islanders marvelled at such love, and said they had not been mistaken in desiring me for their lord; let me at least give them my word that I would return when I had discharged my obligations. I gave it them, and they desired that I should give my hand to the maiden, and kiss her on the mouth; and I am sure that had I wished to enjoy her there would have been no difficulty. The priest gave me three mighty fine carpets, and the maiden two pairs of pillows finely embroidered, and four kerchiefs, and two *berriolas* embroidered with silk and gold. They sent great refreshments to the frigates, and I took my leave; and there was weeping and gnashing of teeth as if it had been the Last Day.

From Estampalia I went to an island which is called Morgon (Amurgo); and there I dismissed the frigate, taking an oath of them that they would not touch the goods of Christians. For among those lands one cannot go about with more than one frigate, and that well armed, with a crew like brethren in friendship, and picking one's way like a crane.

DE CONTRERAS

From Morgon I shaped my course towards the island of St. John of Patmos, where the holy Evangelist wrote the Apocalypse. And here there is the chain with which they took him prisoner.

On the way I fell in with a boat of the Greeks which had on board two Turks, one of them a renegade, who was overseer of the galley of Hassan Mariolo. He had just been married at an island which is called Syra. I put them into irons and dismissed the boat. I asked him whether the fleet was gathering together, since he was one bound to know. He said, 'No'; on which I went on my way and, on inquiring at the city of Patmos, I heard the same news. Here it is bound to be trustworthy, for there is a fortress here which serves as a convent and is very rich. It has ships which traffic with the whole Levant, and they bear a flag like that of the ships of St. John. Upon this I went off to an island which is about fifteen miles away and deserted, and is called Formacon (Furni); my idea being to share out the damask and the money. For that is why I was so loved by my men, because I did not wait till we came to Malta to divide the spoils.

I sent three men up to the high ground to keep

a look-out both on the land side and out to sea; and one of them was to come down with whatever news they might have. Meanwhile I ordered them to put ashore the hatches and the damask. While this was doing, one of the men who had gone up came down and said, 'Sir Captain, two galleys are coming to the island.' I gave fresh orders that the damask and the hatches should be put on board again and I told them to set all hands to the sails and stop them, and leave them hoisted. Soon the others came down and said, 'Sir, we are slaves.' I gave orders that every man should stand to his post, and I weighed anchor and stayed still. I was in a creek. The galleys had not noticed me, to judge from the way they were sailing; for if they had done so, they would have sailed round the island, which was small, one on each side. And so I lay, perfectly still, when one of them rounded the point, under sail. She did not see me till she had gone a good way past. When she saw the frigate, she turned back upon me, for I was very near. The other galley did the same, and they lowered their sails on a sudden with great shouting. It happened that my poop rested against the prow of the galley, and the master, or captain, mounted with a cutlass on to his waist-netting, allowing nobody to come on board, lest he should be upset in the confusion, and shouting, 'Throw the *palamara*, you brutes!' The *palamara* is a cable which the galley wanted to throw over me to hold me fast. When I saw them in such confusion, I said to myself, 'A hundred lashes, or freedom,' and loosing the sheet which I held in my hand, I made sail and drew away from the galley. I hoisted the other sail, and, since both the galleys had their sails caught in their centre gangways, I slipped out before they had got theirs up; and by the time they made sail in pursuit of me, I was already a mile away from them. They began to go to seaward of me, so in order to get out to sea I was forced to pass below their prows. The wind fell, and they chased me for eight turns of the hourglass, without gaining on me an inch. The wind came on again and I hoisted my sail, and so did they and all. They fired their cannon at me, and with one shot they carried away or shot through the standard flying at my masthead, and with another they shot down the trestle-trees in which are placed the mast and the yards. When the lower one came down, I was much afraid that it would sink me; and the more so when the captain of the galley, in

[73]

order to overtake me, made use of a cunning sea-
man's trick, which was as follows: all the crew were
crowding to the prow of the galley in order to see
the frigate, thus preventing her from advancing. So
he made them come aft to behind the third bench,
and the galley began to bound forward and draw
near to me inch by inch. When I saw that I was
almost lost, I set my wits to work. They had won
the seaward berth and I was on the landward side,
so that I was bound either to run foul of her or to
pass across her bows. Now, in this region there is
an island near the mainland which is called Xamoto
(Samos). It has an open harbour, where we are
wont to lie hid with the galleys of Malta, when
trying to capture some prize. I turned the frigate
in that direction, and sent a sailor up to the masthead with a bowl of powder, there to make two
smoke signals, and then wave with his hood in
the direction of the island. When the galleys saw
this, they lowered their sails on the spot and piped
all hands, trying to change their course with might
and main; for they thought that the galleys of Malta
were there. So in a short time we were out of sight
of them. I betook myself to an island which is called
Nicaria (Nacaria), where I lay till nightfall the

next day, keeping a good look-out; for the island is hilly and commands a wide expanse of sea. Then I left for the island of Micono (Mykoní), where I fell in with a French tartan laden with goat-skins, coming from Chios. She brought me word how the captain who had given chase to me with the two galleys – his name was Soliman of Gatanea (Catania) and he had been a slaughter-house man from Genoa – had nearly died of grief at having let the frigate escape from under his very oars. I told him that I was the man; and the master of the tartan was amazed and could not stop talking about it. He warned me that the galleys were on their way to lie in ambush for me when I left the Archipelago. Upon this I resolved to sail for Malta, so I waited for a stiff northerly wind, when I set sail and got away from these anxieties. I arrived at Malta, where they marvelled at what had come to pass; and we shared out the money and the damask, setting apart enough out of the residue for a set of vestments for the church of Our Lady of Grace, which we gave with great content. And by the same token every one was relieved that there was to be no battle-fleet that year.

A few days later they sent me off on a raid with

two frigates, one belonging to the Grand Master and one to my old friend Commander Monreal, with orders to gather information.

I left Malta with the two frigates, which looked like two galleys, and had thirty-seven men in each. I took to the open sea, shaping my course towards Africa, and first touched land at Cape Bonandrea (Ras-el-Halil), seven hundred miles across the sea. I coasted along the salt lagoons and came to Puerto Soliman (Solloom) to take in fresh water. Here, as ill-luck would have it, there were a large number of Moors on their way to Mecca, where is the body of Mahomet.

They laid an ambush for me around a well whither I had to go for water. For all round it are high reed-beds; and as the Moors went naked, and were of the same colour, my men did not see them. Twenty-seven soldiers were going thither with barrels, and sixteen Spanish soldiers with their arquebuses; and while they were at the well the Moors came out from their ambush and fell upon my men. The sailors took to flight, leaving their barrels, and the soldiers fell back fighting. Hearing the report of their arquebuses, I came out with another twenty men to aid them, for by now they were drawing near the coast. And when the Moors saw the reinforcements, they fell back. They captured three of my soldiers, and killed five, whom I could ill spare. Our men captured two, an old man of sixty and another one not much younger. We ran up a flag of truce and bargained over the ransom. I was ready to give them their two for two of mine, and to ransom the third. They said no, I must ransom all three, and might keep those whom I had captured. We left it at that; but they began calling after me to ask how much I would give to have back my barrels full of water. I said that it was not water I needed, but the Christians; but sure it was that I had more need of the barrels full of water than of the men, for I had no vessels left to put it in, save two calabashes, and unless they gave me them, we were bound to perish. So, as if in joke I said, 'What will you take for each full barrel?' They asked for a gold sequin, but even if we had been ready to give them it would have been impossible, because we had taken no prizes. We told them we had no sequins. Said they, 'Then give us biscuit.' I was content with this, and gave them for each barrel, filled with water, a buckler full of biscuit, of which I had good store. I recovered all my twenty-seven barrels, and once more began to beg them to give me the two Christians in return for their men. They would not, and so I proceeded to bury my dead on the seashore. I put a cross over each one. In the morning I found them on the surface of the sand, and was shocked, thinking they had been dug up by wolves. But when I saw them I was horror-struck; for they had no noses and no ears, and their hearts were cut out. I thought I should go out of my mind; so I ran up a flag of truce and told them what a bad deed they had done. They answered that they were taking that offal to present to Mahomet in token of the favour he had granted them. I answered in a rage that I was going to do the same to the two I had captured. They answered that they would rather have ten sequins than thirty Moors. And so, before their very eyes, I cut off the two prisoners' ears and noses and flung them on the ground, saying, 'You can take these with you too!' Then, tying them back to back, I stood out to sea, and threw them overboard before their friends' eyes; and I sailed away, shaping my course for Alexandria. I came across nothing on this coast, and passed on to the city of Damietta, which is in Egypt; and I sailed up the river Nile to see if I

could meet with any cargo-boat. I met nothing. I
sailed along the coast of Syria, which is a distance
of a hundred and thirty miles. I arrived at the
sea-coast of Jerusalem, which is twenty-four miles
from the Holy City. From there I passed on to
Castel Pelegrin (Cæsarea), which is on the same coast;
and from there to Caifas (Haifa). On the point at
one side of this harbour there is a hermitage, within
arquebus-shot or less of the sea, where they say
Our Lady rested on her flight into Egypt. I held
on my course to the harbour of Acre, and there
were ships within it; but they were great ones, and
I had to pass on to the city of Beyrout. I sailed
by there too, and arrived at Surras (Tyre), where
there are two cities and harbours belonging to a
mighty chief, who will barely recognize the Grand
Turk: he is called the Emir of Surras. A brother
of his came to Malta, and was feasted and regaled, and returned home laden with great presents
which the Order made to him; and so our ships
of Malta are entertained and feasted in his ports.
And should these noble Christian princes wish to
undertake the holy journey to Jerusalem, a great
advantage it would be to hold these harbours, and
to have as friends these chiefs, who can put into

the field thirty thousand men, most of them horsemen.

I entered the port of Surras. And when they saw I was from Malta the Governor feasted me – for the Emir was not there – and gave me refreshment.

I went on my way towards Tripoli in Syria, a great city. But I stood out to sea, for fear of bringing out the two galleys which are there. I went off to the island of La Tortosa (Ruad Island, off Tartus), which is off the coast of Galilee; it is a little flat island where there are flowers all the year round. They say that Our Lady and St. Joseph lay hidden here from Herod. I cannot vouch for the truth of it. Here I caulked my frigates, and we ate many young pigeons, for they are innumerable here, and they make their nests in what must formerly have been cisterns. In all these parts, be it understood, I always kept a good look-out; and the signal came that a ship was coming. I went up to look, and it was a Turkish caramuzal. I marshalled my men, and when she came up level with the island, I went out to meet her. She fought hard, as the Turks well know how, and at last I beat her, with the loss of four of my sailors and one soldier; and three of

A MALTESE GALLEY
(From a MS. in the British Museum)

the Turks were killed. I took twenty-eight, living
or wounded, and among them a Jew with all his
shopful of trash; for he was a pedlar. The cargo
was of fine soap of Cyprus, with some linen. I made
all the crew of the other frigate go on board the
caramuzal, and, taking the frigate in tow, returned
to Malta. For I should have needed a big crew for
two frigates; but by this means I remained with my
own frigate well manned. From there I hugged the
shore as far as Alexandretta, where the storehouses
were that we had sacked, and from thence I sailed
along the coast of Caramania as far as Rhodes, in
this wise: from Alexandretta to Bayaso (Bayas),
from thence to the Tongue of Bagaja (the strand
to the west of Lissan el Kahbeh), and from thence
to the Provençal Shoals (Provençal Island); Puerto
Caballero (Cape Cavaliere), Estanamur (to the west
of Cape Anamur), Satalia (Adalia), Puerto Ginovés,
Puerto Veneciano (the Genoese and Venetian ports
are marked on the old charts of the seventeenth
century), Cape Silidonia (Chelidonia), La Finica
(on Phineka Bay). Here there is a good fortress.
Puerto Caracol, El Cacamo (opposite Kakava Island), Castilrojo (Kastelorizo), Siete Cavas (Seven
Capes), Aguas Frias, Lamagra (Makri), Rhodes; and

from thence I went off to the island of Escarponto
(Scarpanto), from which I put out to sea towards
the island of Candia. But while I was out at sea I
was caught by a squall, which made me run for two
days and nights in the direction of the Archipelago.
The first land I met with was an island which is
called Jarhe (Iali), where, they say, lay the body of
either St. Cosmas or St. Damian. The Greeks gave
me refreshment in return for my money, and having
taken it, I took my departure for the island of
Stampalia, where they had wished to find me a wife.
I entered the harbour, and all the town came down
to meet me, thinking I had come to keep my word.
It was simply impossible to land, so I told them that
the galleys of Malta, with which I had come, were
waiting for me at the island of Pares (Paros), and
that I had sailed out of my course to see them and
ask if they were in need of anything. They were
greatly grieved, and gave me much refreshment,
and told me how, after I had left for my last voyage, they had gone with a boat to the island to
fetch Captain Jacomo Panaro, and had brought
him back and feasted him till a French tartan
arrived, coming from Alexandria; and they had
handed him over to her to be taken to a Christian

land, having given him good refreshment and ten sequins for his journey. I took leave of them and went on my way; and in the Gulf of Nápoles, in Romania (Nauplia, in the Morea), I came upon a caramuzal laden with grain, with seven Turks and six Greeks.

I put the Greeks ashore, and went on my way with the caramuzal to the Arm of Mayna, which is not far distant. This Arm of Mayna is a district of the land which is in the Morea, a barren land, and its inhabitants are Greek Christians. They have no houses, but exist in grottos and caves, and are great robbers. They have no elected chief, but they obey him who is the most valiant; and though they are Christians, never, as it seems to me, do they act as such. The Turks have found it impossible to subdue them, although they live in the heart of the Turkish lands. Nay, it is the Turks whose cattle they steal, and sell them to others. They are great archers. One day I saw one of them bet that he would shoot an orange off the head of a son of his with an arrow at twenty paces; and he did it with such ease that I was amazed. They use shields of hide as their bucklers, but not round ones, and broad swords five spans long or more. They are great runners, and have themselves baptized four or five times, or oftener, for the god-fathers are obliged to give them a present; and so every time I passed that way I baptized a few of them.

I arrived at the harbour of Quoalla, for that is what they call it (Porto delle Quaglie, or Port of the Quails), with my caramuzal full of grain. Up came my gossip, whose name was Antonaque – for he was the captain of that people – with his robe of fine cloth, and his damascened knives with silver chains, and his silver-mounted cutlass. When he came on board he at once kissed me. I ordered them to give us to drink, as was the custom. I told him that I had brought the caramuzal of grain, if he would care to buy it of me. He said he would; and we agreed upon the sum of eight hundred sequins, including the boat, which alone was worth more. He said he would bring the money on the morrow, for he had to collect it. But at midnight they cut my cables, by which the caramuzal was anchored, and hauled it ashore. By the time we were able to see the damage, there was nothing to be done, for the boat was already aground. By daybreak there was hardly any wheat left in her, so hard had they worked. Next came my gossip with two others, making excuses and saying it was not his fault; but I knew his people's ways of old. I made as if I was not at all concerned, and gave orders that they should serve breakfast. But while we were breakfasting I bade them weigh anchor, and leave the harbour with my frigate. Said he, 'Gossip, put me ashore.' 'Gossip,' I at once replied, 'I am off to reconnoitre.' And when we were out of the harbour, I said, 'Gossip, off with your clothes,' meaning he was to strip. He said that it was treachery. 'Far greater,' said I, 'is that which you have committed. No more talk, but off with your clothes; and be thankful if I do not hang you at this yardarm.' He stripped to the skin, and they stretched him out, held down by four strong lads, and they gave him more than a hundred strokes with a tarred rope's end. Next I had him washed with vinegar and salt, as the custom is in the galleys, and said, 'Send for the eight hundred sequins, or I shall surely hang you.' He saw that I was in earnest; so he sent one of those he had brought with him, who jumped into the sea and swam, for I would not return to land. He brought the sequins in less than an hour, in the skin of a kid; on which they swam off, for they are fine swimmers. And since that day I have been known in Malta and the Archipelago as the gossip of the Arm of Mayna.

I left there, shaping my course for Sapiencia (Sapienza), and from there I crossed the open sea to Malta, where I arrived in five days; and they were well pleased to see me.

They had already sold the soap and the slaves which I had sent in the caramuzal and the other frigate. They divided up the shares and mine was a rich one, so that my wench could go on building her house. We had also to divide the eight hundred sequins and the seven slaves whom I brought back. We enjoyed ourselves a few days, but not for long; for soon I had to arm, and was ordered to refit my frigate without knowing whither I was going. The fact is, news had come that the Turk was arming a mighty fleet, for what purpose it was not known; so that they were much troubled at Malta, and used their best counsels to put an end to their anxiety, in the following wise.

When the Grand Turk makes ready an armada for outside his own lands, the Jews provide him with a sum free of interest; and when the armada is for within his own lands, they do likewise; only the sum is different. The tax-collector for the district of Caramania and Constantinople resides in Salonica, and we knew that this same collector lay, with his household, at a fortified house five miles from the city; and my lords gave me orders to go and fetch him, as one might go to the *plaza* and fetch a few pears! They gave me a spy and a bomb, and I took my departure in God's name. I came to the Gulf of Salonica, with no small travail, for it is in the very heart of Turkey beyond the Archipelago, which also forms part of Turkey. I leapt on shore with sixteen men and my bomb and the spy, whom I distrusted thoroughly. We came to the house, which is about a mile or less from the shore. I laid my mine and it worked well. We went in and captured the Jew, his wife and two little girls, with a serving lad and an old woman, for the men had fled. I carted them off at once, without letting them take so much as a robe, or allowing my men to take a single rag; and we set out for the shore, where, hasten as I might, I found more than four hundred horsemen, with their horses breast-high in the sea, threatening me with their lances. But they could do nothing, for we were already on board the frigate. They began careering about the countryside, I saluting them with my culverin, which hurled cannon-balls at them weighing five pounds. The Jew offered me anything I liked to ask for, on condition that I let him go in perfect safety. But, although I could have done so, I did not risk it, for he then told me for what place the armada was destined, namely against the Venetians: and they were to demand a million sequins of them, or else they would take from them Candia, which is an island as great in length as Sicily, and lies among the territories of Turkey and in her waters. I consoled him, saying that he was coming to Malta. As I sailed on my course, I fell in with a Greek boat, and when I asked them whence they came, they said from the careenage of Chios. I asked if there were any galleys and they said no; but that Soliman of Catania, Bey of Chios, had gone off in his bastard galley, and had left his wife there in his pleasure-house. Said my pilot, 'I swear to God, we must carry her off to Malta! For I know her house as well as if it were my own; and since Soliman went off last night in the bastard, they will be off their guard.'

I durst not do it, having such company on board. But he heartened me and encouraged me to it. And indeed it was even easier than he had told me. We waited for night; and on the stroke of midnight we landed with ten men. The pilot went up to the house as if it were his own, and knocked, speaking of Soliman like one new come from Chios. They opened to him. We went in and captured without resistance the renegade Turkish woman, who was Hungarian by race, and the loveliest I ever saw. We took two boys and a renegade and two Christian slaves, one a Corsican by birth and the other an Albanian. We took the bed and furnishings, with nobody to say us nay. We went on board and sailed off with the utmost speed, until we got outside the Archipelago, for God sent us fair weather. The Hungarian was no wife, but a mistress. I gave her the highest marks of honour, for she was worthy of them; though I found out that Soliman of Catania had sworn in my absence that he was going to look for me; and, if he took me, he would have me outraged by six negroes – for he thought I had lain with his mistress – and then would have me impaled. He was not lucky enough to take me, though he had my portrait drawn and posted in different parts of the Levant and Barbary, so that if I were taken, these portraits should tell them who I was. I knew they took these away from

Malta when they fetched back the Hungarian and
the boys, whom they had ransomed; but this was
two years later, when he was made King of
Algiers.

Chapter vi

In which is related how I went forth from Malta and betook myself to Spain, where I became an Ensign

∽

I ARRIVED at Malta, where I was received as you may imagine. For on receiving my news everything settled down quietly, and they ceased moving the infantry, which they had sent word to do to Naples and to Rome. This was the Italian infantry, for on occasions like this, the Spanish infantry comes from Sicily.

But a worse fate befell my pilot; for they took him within four months, when he was sailing in a tartan against the pirates. And they flayed him alive, and stuffed his skin with straw, and it is over the gates of Rhodes to this day. He was a Greek, a native of Rhodes, and the most skilful of all the pilots who were in those lands.

About this time, when I was squandering my property, which had cost me so much to win, I came upon my wench shut up with a comrade of mine. And I had been so good to her! I ran him through twice with my sword, so that he lay at death's door. And when he was recovering he left Malta, for fear I might kill him, and the wench fled. But, though I was besought a thousand times by her friends of both sexes, never would I go back to her. And since I had choice enough, the remedy was quickly found, the more so since I was sought after like some high office.

I remained many days, and even months, settled at Malta, which was a miracle, until they sent me to Barbary with a frigate. In nine days I was there and back, towing a *garbo* laden with linen cloth – which almost filled a storehouse – and fourteen slaves. This prize was very profitable to me, and when, a few days later, there came into port a Catalan galleon, which came from Alexandria laden with rich merchandise for Spain, I remembered my country and my mother, to whom I had never written, nor did she know what had become of me. So I resolved to ask leave of the Grand Master, who gave it. me unwillingly, laying his cheek against mine when we parted.

I set sail in the galleon, which was called the *San Juan*, and in six days we arrived at Barcelona. I knew that the Court was at Valladolid; so, without going to Madrid, I followed the Court, for I had learnt that they had been choosing captains. I laid my papers before the Council of War, one of the councillors on which was Señor Don Diego Brochero, who was afterwards Grand Prior of Castille and Leon.

He took a fancy to me, and indeed he had heard about me, and he asked me whether I should like to be an ensign in one of the companies which were shortly to be raised. I said I should; and on the morrow, when I visited him, he told me to go and kiss the hands of Captain Don Pedro Xaraba del Castillo for the favour which he had done me in giving me his colours.

I handed in my memorial to the Council of War, begging that I might be approved; and in consideration of my poor services I was approved.

I was given two drummers, made myself a noble flag, and bought drums. And my captain gave me my commission, and licence to fly the flag in the city of Ecija and the marquisate of Priego. I took mules, and, with the sergeant and my two drummers and a servant of mine, set out on my way to Madrid, where we arrived in four days.

I went and dismounted before the house of my

mother, who had gone for sixteen years without hearing of me. Moreover, when she saw so many mules she was amazed; but I bent the knee and prayed for her blessing, saying to her that I was her son, little Alonso. The poor woman was astonished and confused, for she had married a second time; and it seemed to her that a grown-up son, and a soldier, might not take it well – as if it were a crime to marry; though it was one for her, since she had so many children. I cheered her and took my leave, going to an inn, for in her house there was no room; and even for her and her husband they grudged the room.

On the morrow I dressed myself in brave attire. Attended by my soldiers in their best uniforms – for I had brought them with me – and with my servant behind me carrying my spear, I betook myself to see her and call upon her husband. They wished me to dine with them that day – and God knows if they had enough for themselves! – so I sent down plenty of what was required for dinner. And after it was over, I called my little sisters – for there were two of them – and gave them some trifles which I had brought from foreign parts, and likewise wherewithal to make them dresses; and I did the same for the three others, my little brothers. I gave to all, for I lacked nothing. I gave my mother thirty crowns, so that she thought herself rich. Upon which I asked for her blessing; and on the morrow left for Ecija, enjoining upon her to respect the new father.

I came to Ecija. The town council was sitting. I presented my commission, and went out that they might show me the Tower of Palma on which I was to fly my flag. My drums struck up. I made the usual proclamation, and began to enlist soldiers very peaceably, for which the Corregidor and the gentry showed me great favour.

Now, it is the custom to allow gambling in the infantry regiments, and a drummer-boy took care of the winners' offerings. He would put the money into an earthenware money-box; and in the evening he would break it, and take out what had been put in, with which we bought our dinner.

One day there came into the guard-room – which was in a lower room in the tower, with a grating looking on the street – four stout fellows who had been in there before; and breaking open the money-box they began slowly to count up what there was in it, which came to twenty-seven reals. One of them put them in his pocket, saying to the drummer-boy, 'Tell the ensign that some friends of his have need of this money.' Upon this the drummer-boy summoned the corporal of the watch, but by the time he arrived they had gone away. The drummer-boy found me, for he had come to report it all to me, which he accordingly did. I ordered him to go down to the guard-room and there relate how it had happened. The drummer-boy did so, saying to me as I came in, 'Sir, Acuña and Amador and other comrades of theirs have been here and broken open the money-box, and taken out twenty-seven reals, saying that I was to tell the ensign some friends of his had need of them.' 'Rascal!' said I at once. 'What does it matter if those gentlemen have taken the money? As often as they come, give them all they ask for, as if it were for me; for if they take it, it is because they need it.' While I was saying this, there were many friends of theirs present, who at once went off and told them about it. I heard that they had said, 'What sort of a fool is this poor little ensign!' I began to think how I might punish such impudence, happening, too, in my company. I bought four arquebuses, which I placed in the guard-room, besides a dozen half-pikes which I had; and I let a few days go past, so that the thieves gained confidence and came into the guard-room. I had more than a hundred and twenty soldiers, though a hundred of them were quartered in the marquisate of Priego; and I had twenty with me, veterans whom I maintained. And one day, when the thieves were in the guard-room, quite unsuspecting, I bade my men light their fuses, and take the arquebuses and follow me into the room.

For this purpose, I had summoned the most valiant of my men, and ordered them to fire if the thieves defended themselves; and the rest of them stayed at the door with their half-pikes. I took my spear, and, going into the room, I said, 'You and you and you' – naming six of them – 'you great thieves, lay down your arms!' They thought it was a joke; but when they saw how things really were, they began to try and put their hands to their swords. But the arquebusiers came in with their matches lit, saying, 'Enough of that!' Upon which they laid down their arms. When they had done this, I had them stripped to their shirts and, having leashed them together, I took them off under a full guard and handed them over to the Corregidor, who was Don Fabian de Monroy. When he saw the thieves, he jumped for joy, saying, 'That fellow killed my watchdog, and that one killed a servant of mine.' They were taken off to gaol, and a fortnight afterwards those two were hanged, in spite of the efforts of all the nobility of the city, and there are many of them.

As for me, I was left with their cloaks and swords and collars, with some very good doublets and hose and garters, their hats, and two splendid laced doublets, besides what little money they had; with which I dressed and assisted a few poor soldiers. This was my reward for my twenty-seven reals.

Soon afterwards I heard how, under pretext of begging for alms, certain soldiers – who were not soldiers – were going from farmhouse to farmhouse in the country, stealing. I took my four arquebusiers and a nice mule, and went off to look for them. I heard a report that they were in Cordoba. I went thither, where Captain Molina was raising another company, dismounted at the Inn of the Gratings (*Mesón de las Rejas*), and went off alone to the house of ill fame to see if I could find them by their description, and to see the house. While I was talking with one of the many women who were

there, there came up to me a nobleman's gentleman without rod, attended by a servant, and said,
'How do you wear this jerkin?' – it was of buckskin.
Said I, 'I wear it on my person.' 'Then take it off,'
said he. 'I will not,' I replied. 'Then I will take
it off for you,' said the servant. He was about to
carry his words into effect; so I was forced to draw
my sword, and they were not slow to do the same.
But I was too quick for them, so that I wounded
the Alguacil Mayor, upon which all the women
closed the doors, and the gate of the street as well.
I was left master of the street, which was very narrow,
and not knowing how to act, for it was the first
time I had been in such a house, I went to the gate
of the street. But they turned the key in the lock,
and I could not even find anyone to inquire of; for
they had taken the wounded man into the house, or
else he had gone off, for he must have known the
house. Almost immediately I heard knocking at the
gate, and a little ragamuffin came out and opened it
so readily that I could not tell where he had come
from. The Corregidor burst in with a big crowd,
as you can imagine, and began to attack me. 'Forbear, your worship,' said I, sword in hand. Besides,
whether there had been one or a thousand, it would

have come to the same thing, since no more than one could get into the street at a time. They kept shouting, 'Arrest him!' But nobody was anxious to do it; and there would certainly have been a mishap had not Captain Molina, who knew me, come up with the Corregidor and said, 'Forbear, Sir Ensign.' When I heard his voice, I recognized it, and said, 'Let your worship persuade these gentlemen to forbear. As for me, here I stay.' When the Corregidor heard me called ensign, he said, 'Ensign of what?' And Molina said, 'Of the company which is being raised at Ecija.' 'But is it seemly,' the Corregidor replied, 'that he should come here and kill the representative of the law?' I told him all that had come to pass. He ordered me to depart to Ecija. I at once replied that I would go, but that I had come in search of some thieving soldiers; on which we took leave of each other, and he went off with the captain and his men. I had returned to the inn to arrange for my journey, when one of my four soldiers said to me, 'There are two gentlemen here looking for your worship.' I went out and said, 'What is your worship's will?' 'Is your worship the Ensign?' replied one of them. 'Yes,' said I. 'What do you wish?' Upon which, with his fingers apart, stroking his moustache, he began, 'It is meet one should know men of worth like your worship, and it is meet to serve them. We are sent here by a worthy woman, whose good man was hanged at Granada for bearing false witness. She was left a widow. She has no encumbrances, and is not ill supplied with gear. She was well pleased with your worship, and she prays you to go and sup with her to-night.' As for me, all he said was Greek to me, for I did not understand such terms or such language. 'I entreat your worship,' said I to them, 'to tell me what this lady has seen in me that she should wish to do me this favour.' 'Is it a small thing,' he replied, 'that your worship should have fought to-day like a stout fellow, and wounded an alguacil, the greatest thief in Cordoba?' Then it dawned upon me that she was a woman in the bawdy-house. So I said to them that I esteemed the favour, but that I was on the eve of becoming a captain, and it might destroy my hopes of advancement; though I should have been glad to be without them in order to do as they had asked me. On which I took leave of them and went off to mount my horse. By day-break I was at Ecija. I went to my guard-room and found that my men were quiet, and that there had

been no disorders, which gave me no small contentment.

Three days later, there came a soldier and said
to me, 'Sir Ensign, there is a woman at the Sun
Inn who is looking for your worship. She has come
from other parts, and is not bad-looking.' I went
thither, for I was but a lad, and saw the woman,
whom the host had received in his own apartment.
The girl did not seem ill-favoured, and I began to
talk about where she had come from. She said from
Granada, and that she had run away from her husband, and wished to take refuge with me without
being seen by anybody. She had seemed comely in
my eyes, so I took her to my house and entertained
her, keeping her hidden; and I vow that I was
almost in love with her, when one day she said to
me, 'Sir, I would discover a secret to you, but I
dare not.' I pressed her, and besought her to tell
it to me, and having made me give my word that
I would not be annoyed, she began, 'Sir, I saw your
worship one day so spirited and valiant in the house
at Cordoba, when you wounded that rogue of an
alguacil as easily as in play, that I vowed I would
go off after your worship, seeing that you would
not sup with me that night, though I had sent

certain men of worth to pray you come. And although I have been sought after by many men of renown, since I was left alone, when they hanged at Granada a man whom I lived with, yet it seemed to me that no man might so worthily stand at my side as your worship.' She represented to me that in all Andalusia there was no woman who earned such profits, as the head of the house at Ecija would tell me. I stood dumbfounded when I heard her; but as I was fond of her, all that she said seemed good to me. It even seemed to me that she had given me a great mark of tenderness in coming to look for me and solicit me. Then the Commissary came to call the muster-roll and bring supplies for the company before we marched away. I picked up the men who were in the marquisate of Priego, and in all I numbered on the muster-roll a hundred and ninety-three soldiers. We marched off towards Estramadura on our way to Lisbon, with much content.

I took my wench with me, with as much assurance as if she had been the daughter of a gentleman. And sure it is that she would have imposed respect upon anyone who did not know she had been in the house of ill fame, for she was young and beautiful and no fool.

Chapter vii

In which are continued my Adventures as an Ensign

～

WE were joined by my captain, who had gone from the Court to his own part of the country and stayed there till he heard that the infantry was on the march. He came up with us at Llerena and rejoiced to see so fine a company, saying he was amazed that I had known how to manage raw recruits. We remained very good friends, the more so because I knew how to get round him. Second day's march: orders came that we were to occupy ourselves in Estramadura, without entering Portugal, so we ransacked it from end to end. We arrived at a district called Hornachos, which was at that time full of Moriscoes, with the exception of the priest. While I was staying in the house of one of them, where I had my flag and my guard-room, there came a soldier who was named Vilches and said to me, 'Sir Ensign, I have made a discovery.' 'How so?' said I to him. 'I have my quarters,' he replied, 'in a house where I could get no sort of supper, for they say they have nothing but grape-juice and figs.

But, searching through the house to see if there were any fowls, I came into a room at the very end of the house, where there was a lid in the floor, round like a silo or grain-store. I scraped at it and found it was a sham. I lifted it up and all was dark below. So, thinking that the fowls must be hidden there, I lit a taper which I had in my wallet and went down, for there was a ladder. When I found myself down below, I was sorry I had come, for against the walls were three tombs, all white, and the wall was white too. I suspect that some of these Moors are buried there. If your worship would like us to go and see, there are sure to be jewels, if there are bodies buried there, for these people are buried with their jewels.' 'Let us go,' said I, and, taking my javelin, we went off, the two of us alone, and, entering the house, we asked for a light. The mistress of the house was troubled at seeing me in her house, but she gave us a light, for the master was not at home. We went down into the grain-store, and, when I saw the tombs, I was of the same mind as the soldier, and began to prod them with the point of my javelin. In a moment the slab of wood which was under the plaster came loose, and there stood a great coffer, purposely made of wood, and outside was the plaster, so that it looked like a tomb. It was full of arquebuses and bags of bullets, which was a great consolation and contentment to me, for I thought how with these arms I could equip my company, and how we should be treated with more respect as we passed by. For since we carried only short pikes, and some had not even these, in many places they treated us with scant respect. I opened them all, and they were the same. 'Let your worship stay here,' I said to the soldier, 'until I have reported it to the Commissary.' He did so, and I went off at once and reported it. The Commissary came back with me, bringing his alguacil and his secretary, and when he saw the tombs, he said to me and the soldier, 'Your worship has done a great service to the King. Go to your house and let not a word of this pass your lips, for it is a grave matter.' And to the soldier he said the same. We went back to my house, and the soldier said, 'Sir, my quarters are here, and I have had no supper.' I gave him eight reals, that he might go to the inn, at which the soldier was as glad as if it were a feast-day. I wanted to report it to my captain, but did not do so; for one thing, because I had been charged to keep it a secret, and for another, because I was on bad terms

with him, for he kept on making advances to my
wench.

In the morning, very early, the captain sent me
a message with the drums that we were to march,
which surprised me, for we were to have stayed there
three days. I did as he said, and we marched away;
and just as we were starting the Commissary said
to me, 'God be with you; for upon my word, had
they not held a royal warrant for keeping arms of
offence and defence, that would have been a pretty
business. But all the same, let your worship say
nothing.'

We set out for a place which is called Palomas,
and lay there for two days, and then we left for
another place which is called Guarena, where the
soldiers had a stiff affray with the people of those
parts, so that there were three dead and wounded
on one side and the other. During the fray the
soldiers kept shouting, 'Body of Christ! Had we
only been armed with the arms from Hornachos!'
for the soldier had already told his mates, and even
I had spoken of it more than four times.

The quarrel died down and we departed from
thence; and the Commissary arrived to punish them
within a few days. The Commissary was one of the

captains. I do not tell his name, out of a certain respect. But in the course of this book it will be seen what a dust was raised about these tombs filled with arms. But that must await its due turn.

My captain desired to take his pleasure with the woman whom I brought with me. But, though he had made this known to the woman by messages, he could obtain nothing of her, so good had she become after being so bad. On arriving at a place which is called El Almendralejo (the Almond Grove), after settling the company in their quarters – for it was almost night – I had supper and sent the woman to bed, for she had been with child for two months. The captain sent and summoned me and said, 'Your worship is to take eight soldiers and go to the Alange road, and lie there in ambush, for four soldiers are going to run away by that route to-night, as I know for sure from information given me.' I believed him. And, ordering them to saddle a hack of mine, I set off, leaving the woman in bed. When the captain learnt that I had gone, he came to my lodgings and went in to visit Isabel de Rojas – for such was her name – and after one thing and another, he wanted to lie with her. The woman resisted him, so that she was forced to call for help.

But when the captain saw this, he laid hold of a mallet which there was in the room – for I delighted in the game of mall – and gave her so many blows that the guard and the host were forced to come in and drag him away. She was in such a plight that she was seized with a bloody flux, and miscarried within three hours. I, all unthinking, was in the country, awaiting those who had fled, when I saw it was but two hours to daybreak. 'Gentlemen,' said I, 'let us be gone, for I have had enough of the jest, if it be a jest that the captain has played on me. For if they were going to run away, it would have been early in the night.' I came to my house, and, going into the room, found Isabel bemoaning herself. I asked her what ailed her, and she told me that that evening she had fallen from the donkey, and had been seized with a bloody flux which ended in a miscarriage. Meanwhile I saw that some of the soldiers kept whispering into one another's ears, and this caused me a certain suspicion. I pressed the woman to tell me the reason. I could get nothing out of her but what she had said. I went outside and called a soldier, in whom I had confidence, and asked him if something had happened. He answered, 'Sir, such great knavery cannot be borne in silence. The captain came here and has brought Madam Isabel to the pass she is in, because she is an honest woman. And I vow to God that neither I nor my comrades shall be in the company to-morrow at this hour, for he is nothing to us. It was your worship who brought us away from our homes.' 'Forbear,' said I to him, 'for if the captain has done anything, Isabel must have given him occasion.' 'No, I vow to God. It was rather because she would not lie with him.'

On this I gave orders that they should give barley to my horse, and I put up a portmanteau with a little money and my papers, and went to the captain's house, for day was by now breaking. I knocked at the door. It was answered by a Flemish servant named Claudio. He told me that his master was asleep, and that he could not wake him. I said that there was a post come from Madrid; on which he informed his master, who said I was to wait. He dressed himself, but not entirely, and ordered me to be shown in. I went in and, gripping my sword, I told him that he was a poor sort of gentleman to have acted as he had done, and that I was obliged to kill him. He laid his hands on a sword and buckler; but right is might, and I stabbed him in the breast, with a blow that felled him to the ground. He cried aloud, 'Ah, he has killed me!' The servant tried to help, but it was of no avail, for on coming out he received a slash over the head. I took my horse and went off by the road to Cáceres, where I had some friends, knights of the Military Order of St. John, to whom I told what had come to pass.

They at once informed the Commissary, who came up like the wind; and I learnt that a complaint had been lodged against me, in virtue of which I was condemned to have my head cut off for having tried to kill my captain in his house. For the greatest crime which there is among the military is to be lacking in respect to one's superiors. The complaint was forwarded to Madrid; but everything was in my favour, save my breach of obedience to the captain, who recovered from his wound, though he was in great danger of his life.

I wrote to Señor Don Diego Brochero, and he commanded me to present myself at Court, for he would clear the matter up. This I did by the advice of those knights.

The woman, as soon as she was convalescent, was given by the town council of El Almendralejo

enough to travel from there to Badajoz, and there
find out what she ought to do; for she had had no
news of me for many days. There she plied her
trade in the house of a 'father' and 'mother'; and
it is by no means one of the worst houses in Estramadura.

I came to Madrid, and betook myself to the house
of Señor Don Diego Brochero, who had seen the
complaint at the Council of War and found all the
councillors to be on my side. He ordered me to
present myself at the town gaol, and from thence
address a memorial to the Council, to the effect
that I was a prisoner at the Council's disposal, that
I entreated them to send for and look into the
complaint, and that what I had done to the captain
was not concerned with any matters touching the
service of the King. They highly esteemed this
action, namely, that I should first have presented
myself as a prisoner, and afterwards sent in my
memorial. They gave me a letter for Señor Don
Cristobal de Mora, who was Viceroy or Captain-
General of Portugal, but I did not know what it
contained; though Señor Don Diego Brochero bade
me be content, for I carried good credentials. But
I vow that I went off in a regular funk.

DE CONTRERAS

The companies were going through Estramadura
by easy stages. I went through a few places through
which I had passed before, and the people did me
much honour, for I had always endeavoured to do
good, and not evil. I came to El Almendralejo and
spoke with the alcaldes, and they entertained me
well. I told them I was the bearer of an order from
the King, and asked after Isabel. They said they
had sent her to Badajoz, where she wished to go
when convalescent, and expressed their regret for
what had happened. They told me that on the
following day not half the soldiers were left, for
they had all deserted. They afterwards heard that
he had only twenty soldiers left out of more than a
hundred and fifty; and true it was that he entered
Lisbon with no more than fourteen soldiers and a
drummer.

I took leave of the alcaldes and went to Badajoz,
for my love still endured. I found Isabel earning
money in a house of ill fame. When she saw me
come into it she at once rose and closed the door,
and said to me, 'Ah, Sir Gallant, I entreat a word
with your worship.' She took me into the house of
the master and began to weep. 'Why do you weep?'
said I. And she answered, 'Because I have the joy

[113]

of seeing your worship again. For though I am in this place, I have not slept with a man since your worship was lost to me.' Out came the mistress and said, 'And I can bear good witness to that. For have not more than four gentlemen of the city been treating me, to get me to give her to one of them? But I have been unable to obtain it of Isabel. And sure it is, she was right in showing consideration for a young man like your worship.' 'I kiss your hands for this favour, Madam,' said I; and, talking over our affairs with Isabel, she told me that she had six hundred reals and good household gear; so what would I have us do? I said we would go to Lisbon; and we agreed to do so. I betook myself that night to an inn, and she came to sleep and sup with me. There were some who aspired to her favours, and so desired to give us a bad night. For they brought the Corregidor to the inn, saying that I was the worst bully in Spain. To make a long story short, he broke into our sweetest dreams; and, since a man naked is very different from a man dressed, he began to treat me as if I were a bully, and was for taking me off to gaol. I had to get dressed. As soon as I had done so, I said to him, 'Señor Corregidor, do not molest people until you know them,' and I told him who I was, for he already knew about me, because of the affair at El Almendralejo, and how this was the woman who was the cause of the captain's conduct, and how I bore the aforesaid order from the Council. He was very glad to hear me and make my acquaintance. He craved my pardon, saying how they had told him I was the worst bully in Spain. He asked me to stay indoors at my inn and go off to Lisbon as quickly as I could, and said that if I had need of anything, he would give it to me. I thanked him for this, on which he went away, and I returned to bed. I remained two days in that city, where they stared at me as if I had been a bull, but I did not let Isabel return to the house. The master brought all her belongings to her, in deep sorrow at parting with such a girl. We went to Lisbon with great content, and stayed there more than twenty days, until the companies arrived. At the end of this time my company arrived with four others; and before they had landed I went to present my letter to Señor Don Cristobal de Mora, who showed me great favour and said, 'Go down to meet the ships, and march in with your company.' I said that the captain might do something, for we had not seen each other since I wounded him.

He ordered an adjutant to carry a message to the captain, which he did, and returned, saying that the captain wished to speak to the general. He came to see him, and the general told him to have patience, for it was the King's orders, and my stay with him would soon be finished. We landed the flag, which had been put on board at Alcantara, and marched to the castle, where we called over the muster-roll. And my company was forthwith disbanded, so that the captain and I were separated.

Señor Don Cristobal de Mora gave me leave to go to Court, with a month's pay, upon which I at once set off, with God's help, and came to Valladolid, where I was given eight crowns extra pay to go to Sicily. I went off on active service, taking Isabel with me as far as Valladolid, where she died plying her trade. May God pardon her!

I came to Madrid and saw my mother, and asked her for her blessing. Having obtained it, I set out for Barcelona, and there set sail in a ship laden with cloth and arrived at Palermo in ten days.

In the year 1604 my Lord Duke of Feria was governing this realm. I enlisted in the company of Captain Don Alonso Sanchez de Figueroa.

It was the Duke's wish to arm some galleons and

send them out against the pirates, so, knowing that I was a man of experience, he asked me if I should like to be their captain. I consented, and we sailed for the Levant, whence I brought him a *djerma* laden with the good things of this world, besides another little English galleon which had been engaged in piracy for three years past; and in her were no end of curious things. I omit what happened in the course of this voyage, so as not to bore my readers with more stories about the Levant. With what fell to my share from this prize I provided myself with horses, for I was exceeding rich. I exchanged into the company of the Lord Marquis of Villalba, the first-born son of the Duke.

Chapter viii

In which is related the Loss of the Lord Governor
of Castille at La Mahometa, where I was
present

A N expedition was fitted out for Barbary, with
the galleys of Sicily and of Malta, four from
Malta and six from Sicily, in charge of the Ade-
lantado (Lord Lieutenant) of Castille, who was
General of that squadron; which cost him his life,
as I shall relate. We set out for Barbary with ten
galleys, as I have said above; and those of us who
were in the galleys of Sicily were commanded by the
Governor to leave the body-pieces of our coats of
mail at Messina, in order to travel lighter. We came
to an island which is eight miles from the main land
of Barbary, and is called El Cimbano (Zembra);
and here was held a council of war. It was decided
that we should land troops at a city which is called
La Mahometa (Hammamet), which we had taken
years before with the galleys of Malta. We arrived
within two leagues of the city, on the eve of the
Assumption, in August, 1605, at daybreak. We

landed our men, who went marching across some sand-dunes that are there to the city, where we arrived when the sun had risen and been in full view for upwards of an hour. I was one of the ensigns without a command, who carried the ladders on our backs – for there were seven of us. A squadron was formed of five hundred men, all Spaniards, with pikes and arquebuses, but no breast-plates. We set up the ladders against the walls, with the courage common in such men as these – namely, Spaniards and knights of Malta; and up the ladders we climbed, some falling and others mounting upwards. To make a long story short, we captured the wall, and cut off the heads of the guards in the ravelins, where certain of the janissaries who formed part of the garrison had made themselves a strong position.

The gates were thrown open, and all our men went in, except those of the squadron, which stayed outside – and they must have been another seven hundred men – and I can tell you we had not much room in the streets, which were no more than an ell and a half wide, which is three yards. A few Moors were captured, both men and women, but only a few, for they had hidden themselves in the grain-cellars which there are in every house. There was some grain in the district, which the Governor wished to take on board, and he had even given the order. Outside the town were some gardens with their water-wheels, in which were a few Moors and horsemen – I think the latter amounted to fifteen and the infantry to a hundred; but they were kept in check by the small squadron. The ladders had been removed from the walls, which led to our utter ruin. For after a short time the trumpet sounded the retreat, though by whose orders nobody knew. Upon which every man began to load himself up with the poor rags which he had found, and they set off to return on board the galleys, which had come very close in shore, within cannon-shot. The men began to get on board without further orders. When the Governor was told of it, he said, 'Who gave the order?' Nobody could find out; and they continued on their way, nor could anything avail to stop them; and at last the squadron did the same thing. Seeing that every one was returning on board ship, they broke ranks, by whose orders nobody knew, and fled down to the shore, though not a soul pursued them. And so we found ourselves on the sea-strand, nearly all the twelve hundred of us.

Upon this the Moors who were in the gardens came down by our ladders, which were set up against one of the four curtains that there were in the place, without noticing that the gate in another of the curtains was already open. The Moors hidden in the grain-stores began to come out, and riddled us with their artillery fire from the walls; for we had not even been up to dismount or spike the guns. But if it was God who had so ordained things, how should we have kept our heads? At any rate, we all lost them that day.

At this point arose such a heavy squall that the galleys gave themselves up for lost; moreover, it was adverse to us, for it blew from the sea. The mounted men who were in the gardens, with a few infantry, fell on us as we stood on the seashore, and the carnage was such as is past belief. There was not a man on our side who resisted, though our numbers were almost as great as I have mentioned; while the Moors hardly numbered a hundred, and had no firearms, only lances and cutlasses and short wooden bludgeons. Lo, was not this a manifest miracle, and a chastisement reserved for us by God, whose judgment is righteous?

Of all of us who were there on the seashore, some

threw themselves into the water, and others down
upon the earth, and of these same men so many
fled that I saw a skiff aground, high and dry, with
more than thirty persons in it, who thought themselves safe because they were in the skiff, not seeing
that they were aground and that it was impossible
to push her off with so many men in her – or, indeed, had there been none at all. Many who could
not swim were drowned. As for me, I had got into
the water, all dressed as I was, and it came to a little
above my middle. Over my clothes I wore a coat
of mail, lent me by the boatswain of my galley,
which was worth fifty crowns, and whenever he went
forth to fight in Sicily he armed himself with it. It
weighed more than twenty pounds; and I might
have stripped and cast it off, and swum off to the
galley, although the storm was raging, for I swim
like a fish. But I was so beside myself that I did not
think of this; and I stayed there gaping, watching
how six paltry Moors were cutting off the heads of
those in the skiff; and not one of them resisted.
When they had done this, they threw them into the
sea; they got into the skiff, pushing her off the shore,
and went round killing all those who were swimming about in the water, nor would they take

any back to land alive. Meanwhile they never ceased to fire on us with their artillery and muskets, with which they did us much damage. Sailors had been told off on board the galleys to man the skiffs and collect what men they could; but they durst not approach, for with the squall blowing in from the sea they feared lest they might go aground on the shoals, and be lost on one of them.

At the head of them came the owner of the coat of mail, and he recognized me by a purple cap I wore, which was laced with gold, and my doublet likewise, which was purple too. He shouted to me to strike out to sea, and they would pick me up outside; which I did, without taking off my outer garments — a great piece of folly. I swam as it might have been two strokes, but was drowning under the weight of my clothes and the great storm that was raging. The boatswain, not wanting to lose his coat of mail, went for me and seized me by one arm, and dragged me on board, with a power of water in me that I had swallowed. But there was another poor soldier, who had clung half-drowning to the skiff, and was dragging it shorewards with the surge of the sea, till they cut off his hand to make him let go, on which he was drowned, which filled me with a great pity. But all this was necessary to save the skiff. They took me on to the galley, and there, with my heels in the air and my head downwards, I brought up all the water I had swallowed.

When the Governor saw this disaster, he came down to embark on his own felucca. There was a comrade of his, a captain of infantry, on guard in it. But when he saw this great disorder and the tempest, he made off to the galley. They say that the Governor called loudly upon him by name, giving him the name of 'Comrade.' But I will not tell his name, because of the deed of infamy which he did. For he sailed away, without returning to land, and left his good lord, who was drowned on the spot, while attempting to swim. The skiff of the Capitana took him on board, for they had recognized him. But when they found him he was already drowned. They carried him to the Capitana. I saw him laid out on a shabby carpet, on the poop of the flagship of the Sicilian galleys, dressed as he always was on land, without a wound, but with his face bruised and blackened. And I thought how little it matters whether one be a great lord or a poor soldier; for even the fact that he was General could not avail to save him on that day, when others were saved, though but a few. For of all the infantry which had sailed of the regiment of Sicily, there remained no more than seventy and two; though eight hundred of us had sailed together. The four galleys of Malta lost men in the same proportion, but I never knew the number.

I saw the Governor, as I have said; for there was no officer of my company on my galley, nor had I more than six soldiers with me. So the captain of the galley bade me go to the others, and see if I could find any of our soldiers who might have escaped on one of them. I took the skiff, for it had pleased God to abate His wrath after so many deaths, and after that of the Governor; and the sea was like white milk. And to conquer the place and lose it again, not to speak of the storm, had not taken three full hours.

I came to the Capitana, but did not find a single soldier, save the ensign, for they had all leapt ashore without their colours. And then it was that I saw the Governor, as I have said.

I returned to my galley as it was weighing anchor; and be it noted that within this short time even the shore remained as if so great a carnage had never taken place on it. They would not take any Christians alive, but slew them all, except a few who hid themselves in certain great jars like those in which wine is kept in Spain; for they make them in this country, and there were many of them leaning against a postern gate in this place; but these men numbered under thirty.

Our quartermaster, who was a knight of the Order of Calatrava – and his name was Don Andres de Silva – was taken alive; but after disputing as to who was to have him they cut him asunder, while still living, and gave them half each, which it was pity for us to hear. They cut off the heads of the dead and burnt their bodies, and every one of those whom they took alive had a string of heads hung round his neck and a half-pike put in his hand, with another head stuck on the point; and in this wise they entered in triumph into Tunis. Such was the end of this disastrous expedition. We set out for Sicily, and, on the way, the galleys of Malta turned aside towards Malta, for it was near by.

We arrived at Palermo with the lanterns of the galleys draped in black, and the awnings spread – for it was in August – rowing out of time, which was a sorrowful sight to see. What was worse, so many boats kept coming up asking, one for a husband,

another for a son, or else for a comrade or friend;
and we were forced to answer, 'They are dead.'
And true it is that the wailing of the women made
the very galley-slaves weep.

They carried forth the Governor's body by night
and bore it to a church, with many torches – but I
do not remember the name of the church – and they
left it lying there till it could be taken to Spain.

Proceedings were taken against the captain who
had removed the Governor's felucca, and a brother
of his who was at Palermo in an important position,
seeing from the indictment that he would be condemned to a shameful death, gave him poison one
night; and he was found dead in the morning, all
bloated like a wine-skin. I have said above that I
will not tell his name, for he was very well known.

My company was disbanded, and they sent me
to lodge at Monreale, a league and a half from
Palermo; and there I lay at the house of a baker or
bread-maker, who had a sturdy ambling nag. He
lent it to me every day, and I would go to Palermo
and return to Monreale. At that time I was a fine,
well-set-up young gallant, and envied of all. In the
street by which I entered Palermo from Monreale
there lived a Spanish lady, a native of Madrid, the

widow of a judge (*oidor*), who had brought her
there as his wife. She was beautiful, and by no
means poor, and every time I passed by I used to
see her at the window, and, as it seemed to me, with
intention. I found out who she was, and sent her a
message, saying that I was from Madrid, and would
gladly serve her worship in anything she might
command, for it was more incumbent upon me than
on any other, since I was her fellow-countryman.
She thanked me for this, and gave me leave to visit
her. I did so with much ceremony, and regaled her
with the fruits of Monreale, which are the best in
the realm. From one thing to another we came to
talk of love and marriage; though she had had a
very different position with a man of law and a
judge, living in style, from what she would have
with a soldier who owned nothing but four collars
and his twelve crowns pay, though I was an ensign
without a command. We fell to talking over marriage seriously between us, and I said, 'Madam, I
cannot keep up a coach nor as many servants as
your worship has; though you are worthy of far
more.' She said that it was of no importance; that
she would be content with a sedan-chair, two men-
servants and two maid-servants. On this we sought

a licence from the Archbishop to marry at a hermitage, and he gave it to us; for we did it in secret, which annoyed the Duke of Feria when he knew it, because she had been recommended to him by the Duke of Arcos.

We remained married with great content for more than a year and a half, in love and amity together; and sure it is that so great was the respect I had for her that at times, on our walks abroad, I would not wear my hat in her presence; so greatly did I esteem her. To make a long story short, I had a friend, to whom I would have trusted my very soul. He came in and out of my house as if it had been myself. But so base was he, that despite the great friendship which there was between us two, he began to cast his eyes upon my wife whom I so greatly loved. Although I noticed certain things in him which gave me to think more than usual, I never thought of such a thing; till a page of mine said to me, 'Sir, do people in Spain kiss the wives of their relations?' 'Why do you ask?' said I. And he answered, 'Because so-and-so kisses Madam, and she has shown him her garters.' Said I, 'It is the custom in Spain, for if not, so-and-so would not have done it' (for I do not wish to mention either him or her by name). 'But do not speak of it to any other person. If you see him do it again, tell me, so that I may speak to them about it.' The boy spoke to me about it once again. And in short, though I could not sleep for it, I managed by an effort to appear unconcerned; until, as fate would have it, I found them one morning in each other's arms – and they died. May God keep them in heaven if in that hour they repented. There were many other details, but I am loath to write about it. All I will say is that of all that she owned I did not touch a penny, except the papers relating to my service; and it was her son by the first husband who had the benefit of the property.

VELAZQUEZ: PHILIP III OF SPAIN
(Prado)

Chapter ix

How I went to Spain and there was falsely alleged to be King of the Moriscoes, which caused me much travail

ᔎ

I BETOOK myself to Spain, to the Court, to sue for promotion. I was proposed for a captaincy, and since the position of Sergeant-Major of Sardinia was vacant, they gave it to me, after the Council had deliberated on the subject.

But Don Rodrigo Calderón – God rest his soul! – having desired to chouse me out of it in favour of one of his servants' brother, had it stated in my commission that it was to be held at the good pleasure of the Governor or Captain-General – a thing never seen before.

I spoke to the secretary Gasol about it, but he shrugged his shoulders. I took a mule and went off to the Escurial to speak to the King, Don Philip the Third – God rest his soul! – and he referred me to Don Rodrigo Calderón; but this was no longer in the year 1608. And thus I answered the King, 'Sir, it was Don Rodrigo who had this condition

[131]

inserted in my commission.' 'I will see that your business is dealt with quickly,' said he to me rather irritably. I went to speak to Don Rodrigo, but he had already heard what had taken place between me and the King, and said, 'How do you know it was I who ordered this condition to be inserted in your commission? Come now, come now!'

I went out from thence, and an hour later two men came to me and said, 'Will your worship come with us?' I thought it was a summons in the name of the law, though they carried no staves; and since holding the conversations related above with the King and Don Rodrigo, I was more than ever convinced that it was a matter for the law. And my idea was right. They took me off between them, conversing and asking me what was my object. In this wise we came down to the town, and I thought they were going to put me in prison. But we passed hard by it – for it is on the road – and when we had got about two musket-shots outside the town, the one who was walking on my right put his hand behind him, underneath his cloak. But I looked more at his hands than at his cloak, and at once drew my sword, and gave him such a slash over the head that he fell down on the ground with his writing-case

in his hand, and had I not seen this case, I should
have done it again. The other one, who was the
alguacil, at once put his hand to his sword. But I retired a certain distance and drew a line on the ground
with my sword, saying, 'Let nobody cross this line,
or I will cut him in pieces.' The alguacil mopped
up the blood with some kerchiefs, and in this manner
they notified me that I was not to enter the Escurial
without leave from the King, under pain of death.
Said I, 'And my mule, which is at the inn? Cannot
I go and fetch it either?' 'No,' they said, 'we will
send it to you,' and they went off in great haste to
dress the notary's wounds, and report what had
happened to him who had sent them. I was told
that there was great laughter about it at the King's
dinner-table. A countryman brought me my mule
and I started off on horseback to Madrid. And
during these seven leagues I took counsel with myself, and resolved to go and serve God in the desert,
and never to go to Court or Palace.

I entered Madrid, and betook myself to my inn,
where I persevered in my resolve, and made arrangements for my journey, which was to retire to Moncayo and build myself a hermitage there on the
mountain, and so to end my days.

I bought the necessary implements for a hermit: a hair shirt and a scourge and sackcloth to make a frock, a sundial, many penitential books, some seeds, a death's head, and a little hoe. I placed all these in a great bag, and took two mules and a lad for my journey, but told nobody whither I was bound. I dismissed a servant that I had, received the blessing of my mother, who thought I was going off on service as sergeant-major; and many thought so when they saw me pass by San Felipe, on the road to Alcalá and Zaragoza.

I came to the Arcos gate, where they search you. But when they asked me to open my bag – for they saw it was a big one – I said, 'I entreat your worships not to open it, for there is nothing to declare. What do you think can be left to a soldier coming from Court?' They insisted on opening it, and began by pulling out the implements I have described, at which they stood thunderstruck, saying, 'Sir, where are you going with all this?' Said I, 'To serve another King for a while, for I am weary.' And when they saw that I was going off so well equipped, they were moved to pity, and especially the mule-boy, who cried like a baby. We went on our way talking of my retreat, until we came to

Catalayud, where there were some knights of Malta, acquaintances of mine, of whom I asked the favour of a letter recommending me to the Bishop of Tarazona, for Moncayo is in his diocese.

They besought me not to be so firm in my resolution, for they knew who I was. But failing to move me from my intention, they gave me letters of high recommendation, and also entreated the Bishop to try and put the idea out of my head. The Bishop was a Hieronimite friar who had been the confessor of Philip the Second.

I came to Tarazona and went to an inn, where I dismissed my boy and my mules. He did not want to go, so great was the love he had conceived for me. And two days later I went to see the Bishop and gave him the letters. He desired me to stay and dine with him, and after dinner he gave me a little sermon, laying before me the thousand drawbacks, and reminding me how young I was. I stood firmly to my resolve. I stayed and was entertained for a week in his house, with sermons thrown in, till he saw it was no use; upon which he gave me a letter to his Vicar, who was at Agreda, which is on the slopes of Moncayo. I went thither and delivered my letter to the Vicar, who was amazed at my resolution, and said that I might begin when I pleased.

A great friend of mine was living in this city as Corregidor, named Don Diego Castellanos de Maudes, and when he saw me, he carried me off to his house for a few days, which almost put my idea out of my head. But when they knew my intention in the city, and how the Corregidor was standing surety for me – for he was a man who had been through many dangers – I gained the good-will of everybody. So that when they saw my perseverance they helped me build my hermitage, which was rather more than half a league from the city, on the slopes of the mountain.

I decked it out with a few trifles and a carven image of Our Lady of Grace. I made my general confession in a monastery of San Diego, of the Discalced Franciscan friars, which lies without the city, on the way to my hermitage. And on the day when I took the habit of a Discalced hermit, the Vicar came and blessed the hermitage and said mass, and the Corregidor and many gentlemen were present. But when it was over they went away, and I remained by myself, trying to allot my time to works for the good of my soul's salvation. I put on a robe of the colour of St. Francis and went unshod and bare-legged. I went every other day to hear mass at the monastery, where I was importuned by the friars to become one of them, but I would not.

On Saturdays I would go into the city and beg alms. I took no money, but oil, bread and garlic, on which I subsisted, eating three times a week of a pottage made of garlic, bread and oil, boiled together. But on the remaining days I ate bread and water, and many herbs which are to be found on that mountain.

I confessed every Sunday and received the Sacrament. I took as my name Fray Alonso de la Madre de Dios, and on some days the friars would have me eat with them, desiring that I should become a friar. But when they saw it was no use, they brought an injunction against me to make me give up wearing the habit or frock of their order. They succeeded in this, and I had to change my habit, which grieved me mightily, and adopt the colour of the Victorines. And I believe that had there been any of them in the place, the same thing would have happened. So great was their desire to make me enter into religion.

I passed about seven months in this way of life,

without experiencing any annoyance; and I was happier than a feast-day. And I warrant you that if they had not torn me away from here, as they did, I should have continued there till this day, and had my fill of working miracles.

Let us turn back to the time when I passed through Hornachos, since when five years had passed by, between the years 1603 and 1608, which was the time when I was in my hermitage, or retired to it.

There were certain signs in Spain that there would be a rising of the Moriscoes. The alcalde Madera – and he was a judge of the Council of Castille – went to Hornachos to make certain investigations touching the rebellion which the Moriscoes were said to be plotting. He was sitting with his court in the said place, where he ordered six Moriscoes to be hanged. How it happened I do not know. All I know is that some husbandmen had come to Hornachos from the town of Guarena, to sell something, and saw the Moriscoes on the gibbet; upon which they said, 'So there was something in it when those soldiers who passed through our parts some years ago said that the Moriscoes had a cellar full of hidden arms.' Of course this was overheard and reported to the alcalde, who sent and arrested them. And in the course of their examination they said that a company of soldiers had passed through their parts some years before, and that in a brawl between them and the townspeople, the soldiers had said, 'God's Body, if only they had armed us with the weapons which they found hidden in the cellar at Hornachos!'

They asked them who was the captain. They said they did not know. On which they sent over to the town to see if it could be found out. And since in every town, before proceeding to the billeting, a proclamation is issued in the name of the captain, it was easily found.

Once they knew the name of the captain, who was at Naples at that season, witnesses were found to relate how the soldiers had said, 'It was the ensign's fault. For since he found them, and did not say a word to anybody, he ought to have shared them among us.' Whereupon they endeavoured to find out who was the ensign. Nobody could tell them. So they sent to the Court to inquire who was the ensign of Captain Don Pedro Jaraba del Castillo, during the levy of 1603, and they easily learnt that it was I.

[139]

Inquiries were made about me, and they managed to find out how I had turned hermit and was living at Moncayo, and had renounced serving in the position of Sergeant-Major of Sardinia. For I had written from the hermitage to my mother, and to certain officials of the Secretary of State, who were friends of mine, that position being then held by Señor Andres de Prada the elder, who showed me much favour. Upon this they sent out a royal warrant for my arrest. For it seemed to them that, since I had found these arms, of which no more had been heard up to the present; and since, at a time when the Moriscoes were preparing a rising, I had been unwilling to go and take up my functions in Sardinia, but had retired in the habit of a hermit to Moncayo, which is the strongest point in Spain and communicates with Aragon and Castille, for the frontier between the two lies there: all this made them imagine that I must be the King of those Moriscoes, since they did not know what had impelled me to this retreat.

The bearer of the warrant – whose name was Something-or-another Llerena (an alguacil of the Court) – came and delivered it secretly to the Corregidor of Agreda, and, summoning a large armed force, they went off to my hermitage. And since there was neither a royal road to the hermitage, nor any other, I was amazed to see so many people approaching in a body with arms. I imagined that it was some company of recruits going over into Aragon. But when I saw them advancing on the hermitage, I did not know what to think, the more so because they came on so cautiously, as if it was a fortress which they had got to take. They came up to me as I stood with a rosary in one hand and a stick in the other, and laid hold on me and arrested me. And they bound my hands behind me, and put a pair of shackles on my feet, with the greatest satisfaction, as if they had taken some very strong city. And, placing me on an ass, seated and bound, they began journeying towards the city. I heard people saying, 'There goes the King of the Moriscoes. So that was the piety which made him retire to the mountains.' Others talked all kinds of nonsense, till we came to a place where all the township had come out to look at me; and some were moved to compassion, but the others only to chatter.

They put me in gaol under a strong guard, and there I stayed that night, commending myself to God and examining my life, to discover how it was they could have arrested me with such precautions, under the King's warrant.

I could not have known what was the matter, and so I was of a thousand different minds. On the morrow I asked them to send for the Corregidor. He came, and I asked him to tell me whether he knew the reason of my imprisonment. He answered that he believed it was to do with the Moriscoes; on which I thought it might be because of the arms which I found at Hornachos, which I at once recalled to mind. So I said, 'If it is on account of the arms which I found at Hornachos, why did they take so much pains to capture me? For if I were questioned, I would tell about it.' The Corregidor was amazed, and at once called the man named Llerena and told him; at which he jumped for joy and ordered the manacles to be taken from my hands, for they were torturing me.

They gave me food according to the regulations, but as I had accustomed myself to eat herbs, I swelled up, so that they thought I was dying, and imagined it was poison. They summoned the doctors and cured me; for they at once recognized what was the matter, and it was easy to cure. We journeyed to Madrid, and on the way I was well entertained, but kept my manacles, and had a guard of twelve men with muskets. We arrived at Madrid, and they took me to stay in the Street of the Fountains, in the house of the alcalde Madera, who had come from Hornachos.

When I alighted, the alcalde gave orders to remove my manacles, and showed me into a room where we remained alone. He began asking me affectionately the reason for my retreat, so I told him all that I have written before this. He went on to ask me whether I had ever been in Hornachos. I answered, 'Sir, if it is about the arms which I found there in a cellar, when I passed through with my company about five years ago, let not your worship be troubled, for I will tell you how it happened.' He rose and embraced me, saying that I was an angel and no man, since God had seen fit to preserve me as a light against the evil designs of the Moriscoes. I began to relate to him everything as aforesaid. He ordered me to be taken to the house of an alguacil of the Court named Alonso Ronquillo with six guards, who were never to leave me, but without fetters, with orders to feed me well and to have a doctor at table at my dinner and supper, who would not allow me to eat or drink at my own

will, but according to his, by which I see that a work-
man eats better than a great lord.

Four days passed, during which I was not allowed
to write or send a message to any of my acquaintances, or to my mother. At the end of this time
came the alcalde himself with a secretary of the
criminal tribunal, whose name was Juan de Piña,
and took down my statement *de verbo a verbo*. In
it he would not allow me to call myself Fray Alonso
de la Madre de Dios, but Sergeant-Major Alonso de
Contreras, and thus he made me sign it.

A fortnight later, when I was already in com-
munication with my mother and friends – always
accompanied by guards, but with no doctor at my
table – one night the alguacil Ronquillo arrived at
midnight, in his travelling costume and with pistols
at his belt, and six others similarly accoutred. He
entered the room and said, 'Sergeant-Major, let
your worship dress himself; for we have work to do.'
When I saw him thus equipped, I said, 'What do
you wish, sir?' 'Dress yourself, for we have work to
do.' I had little to put on beyond throwing on my
frock, and when it was done I said to him, 'Where
is your worship going?' 'Whither the Council
orders,' he answered. Thereupon I replied, 'Then

will your worship be so good as to send to San Ginés and fetch some one to hear my confession, for I cannot go forth from here unless I have confessed.' 'It is late,' he answered again. 'Come, for that is not necessary.' From this I feared that it would come to pass as I had imagined – namely, that they would take me outside the town and garrot me.

Chapter x

In which is continued the Collection of Evidence about who was King

⌒

To make a long story short, they took me to the parish priest of San Ginés, which was three houses away, and, retiring into a corner, I made my confession. Would to God that to-day, as I write this, I were a quarter as good as I was then! I earnestly begged and entreated the confessor that on the morrow he should relate all that I requested him to the secretary Prada and my mother; namely, that he should beseech her on my behalf not to let the matter rest, and that never should it be said I had been a traitor to the King. Upon which my confession was ended, and the priest departed, and they put shackles on me and bound me firmly on to a mule; and they fastened my other foot, on which there were no fetters, under the mule's belly.

We went out of the house, – for we had been living in the corner house by San Ginés. They took me up by the way condemned men go to the gallows. We entered the *plaza*, and went down by

the Calle de Toledo and the Puerta Cerrada, by the
street of the condemned. It is true that the road by
which he took me was also the road to the Segovian
gate, through which we had to pass to go to Hornachos. But he might have told me so, in order to save
me the dread I was in, lest they might be taking me
off to garrot me. To make a long story short, we
went on our way for the rest of the night; and at
every shadow of a tree, I thought it was the executioner. By daybreak we were at Móstoles and
went on our way to Casarubios, where we gave our
horses their barley and had breakfast, though I was
loath to eat. I asked the alguacil why he did not tell
me where we were going, so as to spare me such
great affliction as I had endured that night. He told
me we were going to a place whose name he could
not tell me till we arrived there, because he was
under orders from the Council. So I was still left
in some suspicion.

We came within sight of Hornachos, and then he
said that it was there we were going; but that since
justice was to be executed that night, we were not
to enter till midnight. This gave me fresh food for
thought, and we stayed in a garden waiting for the
hour to strike; and I thought it was my last, but I

was not dismayed. Whenever my last hour comes, may it find me as I was then, and I shall be content.

On entering the town, he took off my shackles and unbound me, saying, 'Let your worship show us the house in which were the arms.' 'Sir,' said I, 'I do not know the town, for I was in it no more than an afternoon and a night; and it was night when the soldier took me there, and all this was five years ago. But do you put me in a street which there is in the upper part of the town, where there is a fountain, and I hope, with God's help, to discover the house.' He did so, and I said, 'Either this is the house or that one.' He said, 'Then let us go on to the inn.' We went, and he gave me some supper – a plague on him! A nice supper he had given me, making me swallow all I had done! Day broke; and they arranged a scheme by which I might go into both the houses without exciting attention, in order to recognize the right one. The plan was that I should go into some others first, saying that I was sent by the Bishop of Badajoz to see whether the houses had images and crucifixes, and, since I was a hermit, they believed this. And it caused the image-sellers to come to Hornachos with prints, by which they grew rich. For there was not a door but had two or three crosses, so that it looked like a stricken field. I went into the house and found the cellar; but it was not as I had stated in my examination – namely, that it was as white as a dove, and some thirty feet long and twenty wide.

I stood confounded, and, leaning up against the wall, I kept scrabbling with my fingers, as if in confusion; when, as it pleased God, there fell down a great piece of mud from the place I was scratching, and underneath it was white. I noticed this and said, 'Sir, let them bring someone to throw down a mud wall.' And I scraped all the walls, and only three of them were white, but one was black. They brought a man to throw down the black one, and then the cellar was left as I had said. For out of one room they had made two and thrown a coat of mud over all.

They arrested the owner of the house. He said that he had bought the house two years ago from another Morisco, whose name he did not know. But as they were on their way to arrest this one too, the rumour having already spread abroad that the house had been pulled down, he took a mare that he had and went off to Portugal, and enough it cost to bring him back again! They confiscated his property, which was a piece of luck for the alguacil and the guards. By this time they were already guarding me less carefully. A report was sent to Court relating all I have described, for the alcalde thought much of the news.

I was more or less ill and dying. But with so much medicine and care I was soon healed. They sent for me, and brought a litter to carry me, and a doctor to stay by me, for I was getting better. And in every region through which I passed, the corregidor or alcalde would come out and take charge of me until the next day, when I was once more handed over to the alcalde. And I was most bravely entertained in lovely houses, and not in prisons, for I never entered these. We came to Madrid, and they carried me to the same house. My mother saw me with floods of tears.

I was already well again; and one day they took me to the house of the President of Castille, who was Señor Don Pedro Manso; and there was a conference between counsellors of the Royal Council and the Council for War. Señor Don Diego de Ibarra and his lordship the Count of Salazar were the members of the Council of War; as for the others, I had no acquaintance with them except for Señor Melchior de Molina, who was the fiscal.

They brought the Commissary and confronted me with him. For I had said in my examination that I had reported the matter to him; but he denied that he had been at Hornachos. When they read out my statement, I said that I knew the said Commissary, and that all that was contained in the statement was true; and why did he deny what was so plain? He denied it. So I said, 'Sir, this is the truth; and if it is necessary to maintain it under torture, I will do so.' With this it was all over, and they commanded that I should be taken to my usual prison, and the Commissary to the Court gaol.

Not many days had passed, when one night, after I had gone to bed, they ordered me to dress; and, placing me in a sedan-chair, they carried me to the Street of the Fountains and placed me in a room with heavy hangings, where there was a table with two candles and a crucifix, an ink-pot and pounce-box, with paper. Near by it stood a rack, which I was ill pleased to see; and the executioner, the alcalde and the notary were present. The alcalde encouraged me, but told me how the Commissary denied that I had given him information about the arms, so that it was necessary to put me to the torture; but it grieved him to his very soul. So he commanded them to do what was necessary. The secretary notified me of something – I know not what – which I cannot remember, and the executioner stripped me, and stretched me on that frame, and put the cords on me.

They began by telling me to say to whom I had confided the arms. I said that I referred them to my statement. Said he, 'I know quite well that they gave you and your captain four thousand ducats to hold your tongues.' 'It is a lie,' I answered. 'For my captain knew as much about it as the Grand Turk. What I have already said is the truth.' And after that I would not answer another word during the whole time they had me there, except to say, 'It is a hard case that they should torture one for telling the truth; for it would have been nothing to me to say what I have said willingly. If your worship wishes me to unsay it, I will do so.' His answer was, 'Tighten it and give another turn,' but this time it did not seem to me that it hurt much. Then he ordered that I should be taken down, and placed in the sedan-chair and carried home, where they cared for me and regaled me like the King. And while they were putting me into the chair, the alcalde embraced me.

I stayed in bed and was made much of for more than ten days, and then got up, while the Commissary was closely guarded in the Court gaol. But he was a henchman of the old Constable, who protected him, and of the Count of the Rhine, an old man, besides the thirty thousand ducats which he was said to possess. A warrant was obtained for my release, on my taking a solemn oath that I would not leave the Court until I was given orders. I was bidden to leave off my hermit's habit, in exchange for which they dressed me very finely in velvet, in the costume of a soldier; and every day they gave me four gold crowns for my food and lodging, which the Secretary Piña gave me regularly every four days. All this was paid out of the property of the Moriscoes.

I went out to San Felipe, as I say, gallantly attired. Every one was amazed to see me, and rejoiced that I was set at liberty. I sent every night to the house of the alguacil who had kept me under arrest, and his wife said to me, 'Sir, the Commissary is trying to prove by many witnesses that he was not in Hornachos. For my part, since your worship has eaten bread with us, I would advise you to be gone, and not to fall once more into prison, for, as they say, it is better to take cover than to wait for the prayers of the Saints.' I thought she said it with kindly intentions, and you may imagine that I set about departing as she had advised me. But she did it at the instance of the Commissary, who, as I have said, was rich; and in the end she attained her object.

I had a few savings, and I asked the secretary to give me my allowance for two days, for I had need of it; and having sold my black costume and bought in the Calle de las Postas a dark pair of breeches and an unlined cloak, with some leggings and a bad sword, I left Madrid at nightfall with my saddlebags and cloth cap, by the Alicante road. This was in January; and whoever has travelled those roads in such weather will pity me.

By daybreak I was at the ferry of Bayona, by which I went up country into La Mancha. I arrived at Albacete, from whence I took the road to Alicante, where I arrived in four days. Here I sought information as to the position of the regiment of the Armada, for all the regiments of Italy and of the Armada were in that kingdom of Valencia, where there were many soldiers who had been in my company when I passed through Hornachos. For when they disbanded my company, at the time when I was taken off the active list at Lisbon, all those who remained on the roll were attached to the Armada, in the regiment of that name.

I found out that this regiment was in the Sierra de Cortes and made my way to it at Lahuar, in the costume I have mentioned. In my search for some of my old soldiers, I found means of going every day to see the entry of the companies on guard, among which I found more than fifteen, and among them two who were ensigns on the active list. I related all my troubles to the ensigns, who condoled with me and took me to their lodging. When I told them that the Commissary denied having been at Hornachos, they said that he lied, and that they could even produce proof that he had breakfasted that morning, and in what inn it was. We made some of the soldiers talk, and got them to say what they had to say. And, having sifted it, I drew up a memorial for the legal adviser of the regiment, saying that it was needful for me to collect certain witnesses to the fact that a certain person had been present in a district or town called Hornachos at a

certain time; and that it was of importance to me
for recovering certain property. I added my sup-
plications and gave the names of the witnesses.

By this means I got together five witnesses to the
fact that the Commissary had been in Hornachos
when my company was there. When this was done,
I put it by, and wished to depart. But we were
expecting every day to raid the Moriscoes of that
Sierra, and I waited a few days – in the hope, also,
of fine weather, for it was cruel bad.

Two days after I fled from Madrid, they missed
me, and sent to search for me in different quarters.
They likewise had my name cried in Madrid by
the town-crier. But I made no response, and they
did not so much as know where I was; though they
were aware that I had fled in the direction of
Valencia, by certain traces which they found of me.
Upon this the Commissary began to beg for his release,
on the ground that all I had said was a lie, and that
I had gone back to seek out the Moriscoes and take
their part. He had money, and the two great lords
who supported him, so there was no difficulty about
his release. But the alcalde did not believe any ill
of me; especially as a full inquiry had been secretly
made, even up to the fourth degree, to find out

whether I had any Moorish or Jewish blood. I mention this because the secretary Piña afterwards said to me, 'If your worship owned all that it cost us to make that research and inquiry into your birth, your fathers and grandfathers on the father's and the mother's side, you would have enough to keep you for a good few days. And your worship was lucky that they found nothing of the sort, for if they had done, it is certain that they would have hanged you.'

The worthy Commissary was let out of gaol, and judgment was fulminated against the Moriscoes that they were to be cast out of Spain. As for me, a search was to be made for me.

A few days later, there was a little raid on the Moriscoes of the Sierra de Lahuar, in which I obtained a spirited mule, fit to lead a train. I set out for Albacete, with a passport from the sergeant-major of the regiment, to the effect that I was not attached to any regiment, and that I had won the mule, and it was mine, with a description of it. I entered Albacete and sold the mule, and they gave me thirty-six ducats for it, though it was worth a hundred.

I went on my way to Madrid, and before I had

travelled a league, at Vallecas, I folded an envelope with the superscription, 'To the King, our Master, by the hand of the secretary Andres de Prada.' I entered Madrid at nightfall with my saddle-bags, like a letter-carrier. I went straight to the house of his lordship the Count of Salazar, and had speech with his Secretary Medina. But when he recognized me, he bade me begone in God's name, for if they captured me, I should surely be hanged on the morrow. I argued the point, but he repeated that I must begone. I summoned a page and said, 'Let your worship tell the Count that there is an express arrived from the army of Valencia.' He at once ordered me to come in, but when he recognized me, he looked all round him to see if anybody was about – in order, as I thought, to have me arrested. Said I to him, 'Sir, I am Ensign Contreras, and it is to save my reputation that I am forced to come in this plight' (for I had arrived with mud up to my knees); 'and in order that your lordship may see how things stand, I bring with me a report sufficing to prove that the Commissary was at Hornachos; and how in order to go and prepare it where there were soldiers of my company, I departed without leave. And now will your lordship give what orders he may deem suitable.' Then said he, 'By the habit of my Order, I had always thought well of Contreras. Go to the house of Melchior de Molina, the fiscal, and tell him your story at once; and we shall consider it to-morrow.'

I betook myself to the house of Melchior Molina, the fiscal, and they told me he was in bed; on which I determined to go to the house of a woman of my acquaintance. When I knocked at the door, I was answered by a servant of hers, who opened it. When she recognized me, she shrieked, as if in terror, 'Why, it is the ensign!' I went in, in the plight I have related, so that it was hard to recognize me, and said, 'What is all the fuss about?' 'You are mad to come to Madrid,' the woman answered. 'For they will hang you as soon as ever they catch you. By the wounds of God, make haste to a church.' Said I, 'Isabelilla, take this. Go to the house of the Ambassador of England, and bring a pasty, or whatever you can find, and some wine, for I am dying of hunger. If I am to be hanged, let me at any rate die with my belly full.'

The girl was there and back in a twinkling. She brought the pasty and the wine, and I said to her mistress, 'Sit down and sup.' She said that she had

had supper, so I began mine; and when I had finished, I had them wash my feet with a little wine, and went to bed. I slept, for I was wearied with travel. But, early as I rose, the fiscal had already gone out. They told me he had gone to Mass at the Jesuit church, and I went thither. As he came out of church, I spoke to him, and told him how I was the bearer of a report, and how the Count had told me to take it to him; and that they would see each other at the Palace. He took the report, grieving to see my plight, and told me to wait for him in his house. And I did as he commanded me.

The servant of the lady in whose house I had supped was the mistress of a bailiff, and told him about it in the morning, while I was away at the fiscal's house; for I myself had said I was going thither when I went out in the morning. He told his master, who was an alguacil of the Court named Artiaga; and, making themselves ready, he and some other bailiffs went to wait for me as I left the house. I waited until midday, when the fiscal arrived. As he alighted from his coach, he saw me, and said, 'Come, your worship, for His Majesty wishes to confer a great favour upon you.' He said this grasping my hand. Those who accompanied him were amazed to see him use such ceremony towards a man who looked like an unmounted letter-carrier, or meaner still. We went into his study and sat down, and he began to extol my merits and said, 'Go, your worship, to the house of the Count, for we have been together at the Palace, and have passed a resolution touching your worship.'

I went forth from the house, whereupon the alguacil and his bailiffs fell upon me with shouts of, 'In the King's service!' I grasped my sword and began to make play with it. It seemed to me that it was a trap laid by the fiscal, so I let nobody come near me. They told the fiscal, so he came out to the door, saying, 'Rogues! Thieves! What are you doing? Do you know who this is who goes dressed as a letter-carrier? By the King's life, I will have you thrown into a galley. Was it not enough that he was leaving my house?' At which the alguacil stood bewildered, and, sheathing my sword, I betook myself to the house of the Count, with more than a hundred persons before and behind me. I awaited his arrival; and the people had not yet gone away from the door when he arrived, and said to me, 'Come upstairs into my house, Sir Ensign.' I followed him, and when we had gone upstairs, he said to me, 'Your worship has behaved like a most honourable man. The business is at an end. Bethink yourself where you would like to have a company, and you shall be given a commission.' I kissed his hand for this and said, 'Sir, since it is to be, let it be for Flanders.' He then gave me a note to the Secretary Prada, and with it three hundred reals in pieces of two. Upon this I betook myself to the Secretary's house and presented the note; and he folded and gave me an envelope for the King, who was at the Pardo. I went on to the Pardo and handed the envelope to the Secretary; and he said I was to come back to his office in the evening at nightfall. When I came back, he gave me an envelope for Secretary Prada in person, with a thousand reals in pieces of four. I took both the one and the other, and came to Madrid, and handed over the envelope, and in it there was a commission for Flanders, with extra pay of twelve crowns, and a letter for the Archduke, in which the King commanded him to give me a company of infantry. So I dressed myself as a soldier and followed the route to Agreda, where I had been a hermit, after asking my mother for her blessing, and leaving her some little help out of what had been given to me. As for the Commissary, since he had money and such good guardian angels, and had, moreover, already been released on parole – besides which, judgment had been pronounced against the Moriscoes expelling them from Spain – he was only given a term of banishment, which cannot have lasted long, for I saw him at Court not much more than four years later.

Chapter xi

In which is related the Departure which I made from Madrid for Flanders and what happened at the Death of the King of France

~

I WENT forth from Madrid and took the road to Agreda, where I arrived in a very few days. I went to an inn, and all the town knew that I was there, and their delight at seeing me was infinite, especially because of the honourable commission which I held from the King.

I lay there five days, and then took my departure for San Sebastian, where I arrived in safety and set sail in a ship of Dunkirk for Flanders, where I arrived in eight days. I landed and went on to Brussels. I presented my commission to the Archduke, who did me much honour, and ordered me to enlist; saying that on the first opportunity they were to give me a company. I did as he said, and enlisted in the company of Captain Andres de Prada, who was related to the Secretary of State, and the regiment of Quartermaster Don Juan de Meneses, which garrisoned Cambray.

PONTIUS, AFTER RUBENS: THE INFANTA ISABELLA
(British Museum, Print Room)

For more than two years no opportunity arose for going out on campaign, or for giving me a company, until the affair concerning the Princess of Condé was settled – whom the King of France, Henry the Fourth, was demanding in any case; he knows why. This same lady had been received into favour by Her Highness the Infanta, and she kept her under her authority at Brussels, together with her husband, who is the Prince of Condé, and who took the oath of allegiance in France as Prince with that style; and he was the legitimate heir to the crown of France, if the great worth of Henry the Fourth had not taken it from him. And now is the moment to relate a marvel concerning the King, of which I was a witness, and I have also given an account of the matter before the magistrates of Cambray.

Be it known that the King of France had formed his league with the potentates of Germany and Italy, with which the reader will already be acquainted, for it was that of the year 1610, and I believe that it is still in existence even to-day.

He was on his way to St. Denis (San Deonis) to receive the Queen's oath of allegiance, for he left her in that town. On the day when he had done so, he was on his way back to Paris. It is two leagues from any high road; and as he entered the city, being in a narrow street where the guard could not close round the carriage in which the King was driving, a man fell upon him and stabbed him with a butcher's knife. When he saw that the King was speaking, saying, '*No le a tué*,' which means, 'Do not kill him,' he fell on him a second time and gave him another blow, by which he slew the most valiant King that has existed for two hundred years past in those parts. They arrested that man, to whom they gave tortures without end until he died. But all that he ever said was: '*Mon Dio de paradi*,' which means, 'My God of Paradise.' Moreover, when they asked him who had directed him to do it, he said, 'Nobody,' but that he had done it of his own accord, so that the Christians might not suffer, and that he had come from his country twice before to do it; but he had not found an opportunity, and so had returned, having spent what he brought with him.

This man was called Francisco de Rubillar (François Ravaillac), a native of Angoulême, and he was a schoolmaster. Angoulême is in Brittany. This took place on MAY 14, 1610, at four in the afternoon. All this is a true story, for since I was at Cambray, which is near by, I verified it all. But now I will tell what I saw, as I mentioned above.

As I have said, I was in garrison at Cambray with my regiment. Orders had been given that it should prepare to go out on campaign; and we soldiers longed for this as we did for salvation.

It happened that I was appointed to go the round of the walls with another ensign, a Majorcan, named Juan Jul, for our company was on guard. We went up on the wall, where there are several sentry-boxes. When we got to the top of the Péronne Gate, we heard a letter-carrier's bugle, at which we rejoiced. Now, you should know that the postmasters leave six horses outside the city for the letter-carriers who pass by; but they cannot be given to anyone unless he produce a warrant from the Governor. This is given them in a little box, which moves on cords from the land side to the other side of the moat. The letter-carriers come to that point and hail the guard, who asks them from whence they have come. If they bear letters, they throw them into the box, from which they are taken to the Governor's house. The Governor issues a warrant, which is taken and thrown into the box; and, having pulled the cord, the letter-carrier takes the warrant, and gives it to the postmaster, who gives him horses.

The letter-carrier hailed us, and we answered, 'Whence do you come?' He said from Spain; for Cambray is on that road. We asked him, 'Do you bear letters for the Governor?' 'No,' he said. 'Let me get on at once.' On which we asked, 'What news is there?' 'This evening,' he answered, 'the King of France was murdered by two stabs of a knife.' On this we decided that I should go and inform the Governor, since I was the most active of them. I arrived, and he was in bed; and when I told him the news he was thunderstruck, because he knew in what a critical state matters stood.

He gave me the warrant, and I went up on the wall. We threw it into the box, and the letter-carrier took it, for he was on foot, and had brought only one horse. He went straight off with it to the postmaster, who lived a musket-shot away.

We continued on our rounds, giving news of what had happened to all the guard-rooms; and every one was shocked. Day broke; and the people were coming in from the whole of the Cambrésis, in which there are many towns, bringing in their goods in carts to leave them in Cambray; for they said that the people would rise and pillage them on account of the death of the King. And yet this story of his death was a lie, and I became a laughing-stock. All this happened as has been related. But at the end of nine days there came riding post-haste a servant of the Ambassador Don Iñigo de Cardenas, who was Ambassador of our King in Paris. He described the murder as it was told above, without differing in any point; and how the Ambassador's house was left with two companies to guard it, for the Queen had told them to place them there, so that the Ambassador and his people should not be murdered; for people might think he was the cause of the murder.

They marvelled at the coincidence, and sent and called the postmaster, so that he should tell whether he had given the horses that night; and he said, 'No.' Upon this we were ordered to relate our stories as we had told them; and the belief was that that letter-carrier had been either some devil or some angel.

We went out on campaign and remained until September, when we returned; and I asked leave of the Archduke, for I had heard that there was a Chapter-General at Malta, where I hoped to gather some fruit from my labours; as indeed I did.

He gave me leave; but as I had not the means to

go on horseback, with a servant or alone, I dressed myself in a pilgrim's habit, in the French style, for I spoke the language well. I hid a sword in my staff, and my papers in my wallet, and set out on my journey. I passed through a town which is called Creil, which is between Amiens and Paris, where the Prince of Condé was staying with the Princess, who had now gone back without fear. I begged her to grant me the favour of a letter to the Grand Master at Malta. She gave it me, and it was of the length of a finger, and as slender; and with it she gave me three hundred reals. I went on my way and entered Burgundy, and I came to a city named Jalon (Châlons), where a river flows beneath the walls. The gate to which the road led along which I had come was shut, so I had to go along the river-bank in order to enter by another; and as one curious of such matters, I walked along looking in admiration at the fortifications. This attracted attention, and when I entered the gates they arrested me. Since I had done nothing, I would not give up my staff, and resisted. And they kept saying, 'Spanish dog! Spy!' for we cannot disguise ourselves, try as we may. During our struggle the staff came unjointed, and they saw my sword, which further convinced them that I was a spy. They took me to gaol, where there was some talk of putting me to the torture, and some were of opinion that I should be hanged; for since I had been found with concealed arms, what further proof could be required? I showed my papers, and the Archduke's leave of absence. But not even these were of any avail, until a Spaniard who had married and settled there – for he might not remain in the King's dominions, because he had been one of the Flanders mutineers who had been proclaimed traitors – had pity on me as a fellow-Spaniard, and came and said to me, 'Sir, your worship should be on your guard, for these people wish to hang you. Look now, if you wish, I will do what I can.' I thought he was in jest, until I saw that it was a serious matter; and it drove me mad to think that I should die all unprepared as I was. 'Sir,' said I to him, 'I have here a letter of recommendation given me by the Prince of Condé for the Grand Master of Malta, from which they will see that I am going on my own business, and am no spy.' 'Let your worship give it to me,' he said. Body of God! It was so small that I could hardly find it; but he took it and laid it before the magistrates. I remained in low spirits, as can be imagined. But an hour later I heard a great bustle in the gaol, and I thought they were coming to wreak their cruelty on me, especially when I heard a shout of '*Du eté lo español?*' which means, 'Where is the Spaniard? Fetch him out.' I went out, and there were all the magistrates, and they said to me in French, 'Come with us,' and they took me to an inn, where they gave orders that I should be well entertained. The host, who was no more a heretic than Calvin, did so. On the morrow they gave me two light horsemen to accompany me as far as the French Leon (Lyons) and a horse for myself; so that I did not spend a penny till I arrived there, and ate all the while of the best.

At Lyons they handed me over to the Governor. He did the same thing. For after I had been entertained at an inn, two other light horsemen escorted me as far as the territories of the Duke of Savoy — Chambéry was the place. I went on my way, and from thence I took the road to Genoa, where I set sail for Naples, and from thence to Palermo, where the Duke of Osuna was Viceroy. I had audience of him, and he ordered me to be given a hundred ducats towards my expenses, because he saw that I was the bearer of a written leave of absence. There were those who said that he had given orders to have me arrested for the murders I had committed in the past; so, without finding out whether this was true – and it was not – I set sail, and went to Malta, where I was very well received. They at once sent me on ahead in a frigate to collect information, while our armada was on its way to the Querquenes (Kerkenneh Islands) off Barbary. And this was in the year 1611.

I made my voyage, and brought back a true report. A Chapter-General was held, at which they received me into the Priory of Castille, exempting me from the obligation of passing the necessary tests. Nobody voted against me in the whole Chapter, though there were more than two hundred of them. I completed my year's novitiate; and at the end of it they gave me the habit of the Order, though certain knights brought it up against me that I had committed two public homicides. But I took the vows notwithstanding, by order of the Grand Master. During my year of novitiate, I had a dispute with a presumptuous knight of the Italian langue. It was for taking the part of another who had done me a good turn. They fired their pistols at me twice, but did not hurt me. I asked for leave to go to Spain. I went in the galleys of the Order as far as Cartagena, without spending anything on food, in the company of the knight with whom I had had the dispute. But there would not be paper enough in Genoa to relate all that came to pass.

This knight took me as far as Madrid, where he left me. Here I stayed, wearing my habit; and every one gave me their congratulations, some out of envy, others out of love.

I petitioned the Council of War for a company, and they sent me to serve in the Royal Armada, where I was present at all that happened until I returned to the Court on leave. At this time I took a fancy to a married woman, and we were lovers for a few days. But another woman I knew, who was also married, told tales on me out of jealousy, so that she forced me to do a vile action — for such I take it to be. It was as follows: I went to her house, in her husband's presence, determined to slash her face; and I got out my dagger to do so. When she saw my determination, she hid her face, bending down her head till it was between her legs. I was so savage that I turned up her skirts — for she was in a suitable position — and slashed her twice, as if she had been a melon. Her husband seized his sword and came out after me; for it was in the shop where he worked, and he was a journeyman. And since there are many officials of the law in Madrid, he at once charged them to arrest me. I took refuge in a house, where I took up a strong position at the door, and let nobody come in, save on the point of my sword. There were police of the town and of the Court there, and the longer it went on the more of them came; so much so, that they called one of the alcaldes of the Court, a certain Farinas. He came up with a great troop of alguacils and, taking off his hat, he said, 'I entreat your worship to put your sword back in your belt.' 'Your worship entreats me with such courtesy,' I replied, 'that I will do so, if they were to cut off my head for it.' When I had done it, he said, 'Let your worship swear on this cross not to take to flight, but to come with me.' 'One who has done as your worship commanded has no need to do so,' I answered. 'Your worship may lead me wherever you please.' We went off in a friendly way, and came to the town gaol, and he said, 'Your worship will remain in safe keeping here, until the Chapter and His Highness the Prince Grand Prior are advised of it. You there, tell them to give him a room, the best you have got;

and God be with you. I will come and see your worship to-night.'

The gaoler said to me, 'If your worship would like to be in an apartment with some Genoese knights, you will have company.' I said that I would, so he went up and told them, and they readily consented.

I at once informed the secretary of my Assembly, but they already knew about it. The Genoese knights gave me supper, and told them to make up a bed on the ground, which was not a bad one; and at twelve o'clock at night came the alcalde to put a thief to the torture, and on his way there he proceeded to examine me. I replied that his worship well knew that on the day I had assumed my habit and taken the vows, I had laid aside my freedom, and so I was not at liberty to plead before his worship. But I besought him first to hand me over to the Prince Grand Prior as my judge. 'You say this,' he said, 'at the risk of Heaven knows what consequences.' But I answered, 'What I have said I stand to, and sign it with my name.' Such was my statement, on which the alcalde went off and I went to bed.

In the morning the alcalde came in great haste

and told me to dress, for the whole court was waiting for me. I answered that those gentlemen were not my judges, and so I would not go. He went off to tell them this, and they ordered eight galley-slaves to come up and take me into the court, bed and all. This was at once carried out, and they planted me there, just as I had lain in my room. They began by saying what is customary in that tribunal. I answered with such a word that they were forced to order me to be taken to the cells. But as I was going along the corridors, I met two knights of my Order and the fiscal, coming with an order from the Assembly to demand me. They went into the court, and it was decreed behind closed doors that an alcalde should be sent to report to the Council. One of them went, named Something de Valenzuela, and he was admitted into the King's presence. He returned at midday – during which time nobody was examined – bringing with him a decree, of which I possess a copy.

It says: 'Let Ensign Alonso de Contreras be handed over to the Prince Grand Prior, my nephew, with all that he may have written by his own hand, on condition that it be first ascertained whether he has taken the vows; and if he have, let a copy of his certificate of profession be left in the hands of the alcaldes.' He came back with this, and they summoned me – for I was already dressed – and asked for the certificate of my profession. I sent for it, and, after examining it, they handed me over to the knights and took me to the royal gaol, where I remained until the Assembly banished me for two years. I went and served in the fleet, remaining there until I once more asked for leave to go to Court and solicit a company.

An election of forty captains took place, but the lot did not fall on me. I left Madrid resolved to betake myself to Malta; for it seemed to me that there I might prosper. I came across a knight who was going to Malta, and we went off together. We came to Barcelona and set sail for Genoa, and on arriving at that city we left for Rome by land, and arrived in a short time. Here I met with a slight mishap, for I fell ill of a tertian fever. But since I was able to get up, one day I went to pass the time at the house of some Spanish women. Two Italian gentlemen arrived and came upstairs, for the servant had let them in without the knowledge of their mistresses or of myself. On entering the room, they asked me what I was doing there. I answered that I was talking with these ladies of my country, for we came from the same parts. They said to me shortly, 'Come, be off.' It seemed to me that it would be an indignity to depart in this wise, so I pretended not to understand, but went on talking to one of the ladies. Again they spoke to me, saying, 'Are you waiting for us to throw you downstairs?' I could stand no more, so, raising the sword which I was carrying in my hands like a sick man, I struck them, so that they both rolled downstairs, one of them with his head badly wounded. On hearing their cries, the police rushed up – for there are many of them in that city – and, putting us all into a carriage, they took us to the Governor's house, where matters were explained; upon which the women, and even the men themselves, bade me give them my hand. And thus we departed, each man to his own house.

These men had not the courage to kill me, so they got together with my landlord and bade him tell me that if I wished to be healed of those tertian fevers, there was a doctor who would do it in four days, and would accept no money till I was well. I longed for health, so I told him to fetch the man. On the morrow the host entered and said that he was there. He came in. He was a man in clerical dress, and he examined me and questioned me about my illness. I told him about it; and he answered, 'In four days I will give your worship health. God be with you, for to-morrow I will return. Do not rise from your bed.' He went away; and the host said to me, 'He is the best doctor in Rome, and body-physician to the Cardinal de Joyeuse.' I waited till the morrow, when the good doctor, or devil, came and produced a phial of red wine, and a paper with some powders. He asked for a glass, and poured several of them into it with some wine from the phial, and, stirring them together, he said to me, 'Drink it up, your lordship.' I did so, and when I had finished drinking, he told me to wrap myself up, for I was already well. He went away; and within half a quarter of an hour my jaws began to be rigid and my bowels to gripe; and, calling for a confessor, I began to throw up in convulsions all that was in me, at the same time evacuating inky excrements. The knight, my companion, rushed off to the house of the Spanish Ambassador, and summoned the doctor, a Portuguese, who came immediately. When he had heard what had happened, and seen what I had thrown up and evacuated, he prescribed medicines by which, with great difficulty, he stopped this grave malady. He afterwards said that, to show how robust my stomach was, he would not like to give a mule as much of the powder as is contained in a walnut-shell, which would be the end of him in an hour; whereas I had been given a heaping silver spoonful of it.

He went on till he left me healed. But when he wanted to have the doctor arrested, the host said that he did not know him; for he had come to the house to offer his services, saying that he was the doctor of the Cardinal de Joyeuse, and had done it for my good. But no such doctor ever appeared or returned, so that I believed he had been sent by those two who had rolled downstairs. We let the matter rest at that, and when I had got well I left for Naples with my companion, going from thence to Messina, and then to Malta.

Chapter xii

How, being come to Malta, I returned to Spain
and became a Captain in the Spanish Infantry,
with other Events

HERE I found letters from Spain, and they were
from the King. One was for the Grand
Master, in which he was ordered to give me leave
to go and raise a company of Spanish infantry,
which had fallen to my lot by the promotion of eight
captains who had obtained advancement. The other
was for me, from Señor Bartolomé de Anaya, who was
one of the lords of the Council of War, informing
me of my promotion. I made arrangements for
my departure, which took place within a fortnight.
The Grand Master recommended me to pass through
Marseilles on my way, and give notice to two of the
galleys of the Order that they were to pass in all
secrecy to Cartagena and take on board two hundred thousand ducats, which had reverted to the
Order during the vacancy of a commandery.

I went on to Barcelona and to Madrid, which
took in all twenty-seven days from Malta. When

I arrived, the companies had already gone out to raise levies; and as for mine, it had gone to Osuna with a cousin of mine, an ensign of Flanders, to take charge of the levy. For since he had not obtained a company, he wished to raise mine in my name, with the rank of Ensign; and if I did not arrive in time to embark, since I was so far away, he was to remain with the company. This was the Council's doing. But I made such good speed that I arrived more than four months before they sailed, which they did for the Philippine Islands. I left Madrid for Osuna, which I entered by post with my commission, which they had given me in Madrid. When my cousin saw me, he turned as white as death, for he thought himself as good as captain.

We talked with each other. I offered him all that is due from a good friend and relation. He said that he desired to go on the expedition. I thought highly of him; but I did not know his damnable intentions. For he led astray a boy whom I had as lance-bearer, and induced him to give me corrosive sublimate to kill me. The first time he gave it me in two soft-boiled eggs, taken out of the shells and powdered with corrosive sublimate and sugar. I crumbled bread into them, as was my wont, and ate them. When an hour had gone by, I felt sick unto death and began to vomit. They sent for the doctors and made me confess at once, for they thought I should die that night; and all the town was sorry for me.

At midnight they gave me a rich cordial. But the boy, who had gone to fetch it, poured into it ten maravedis' worth of sublimate, so that, as I drank, it made four sores in my throat, and I could not finish it. The doctors were beside themselves, and went to the apothecary's shop to ask what he had put into it. He answered, 'What was in the prescription.' They gave me something to make me vomit, but it was not necessary, for nature did this without medicine – which was my real cure. Day broke, and the Governor came to see me, with the best people of the town, and ordered that they should prepare my dinner in his house; and without my knowing it, he had them arrest a woman in my house. Dinner-time arrived, and the boy went to fetch the dinner, and poured into it another paper of sublimate.

I ate it, and then began my usual vomiting, which they thought came from the previous meal. And

I brought up all my dinner, so that not a trace of it was left in my body.

There was a soldier whose name was Something-or-another Nieto, who was keeping the flies off for me, for it was August. He was a little unwell in the lower regions, so he said, 'Give what is left to Nieto, for he may well eat it, though it is Friday.' The poor man ate it, and at five in the afternoon he was dead.

During all this time my relative the ensign had not been in to see me. But the boy went to the house of an alcalde, to whom I had transferred the property I possessed, which is as good as a will, and who had in his keeping the key of the chest. 'Sir,' said he, 'my master says, will you give me the key to take out an indulgenced bead for his rosary, which there is in the chest,' and this was the truth. The alcalde gave it him; and he took out six hundred reals and a great Maltese cross weighing 250 carats, and stockings and garters and ribbons, nor did he appear throughout all that day; till the alcalde came to see me and asked how I was feeling. I said 'Better'; and the reason was that he had not gone on giving me the corrosive sublimate.

He inquired about the bead, desiring to know

what indulgences it carried with it. 'What bead?' said I. He answered, 'Did not your worship send the page for the key of the chest to get it out?' 'No, sir,' I said. 'Well, I gave it him,' said he. They went to look for him, and found him in the house of a muleteer; and he had made all arrangements to go off to Seville. They brought him before me, and when I asked him for the key of the chest, he produced it. On opening the chest, they found it minus what has been enumerated. I asked him where he had put what was missing. He said he had hidden it. They went with him, and brought it all back save twenty-six reals. On which I said, 'Search those pockets of his.' They did so, and found on him a paper of corrosive sublimate. When they opened it the landlady said, 'Why, sirs, this is the poison they were giving the captain!' When they discovered that it was corrosive sublimate, I said to him, 'Traitor! What have I done to you, that you should have wished to murder me with this poison?' 'I found this paper in the street,' he answered. 'Sir,' said I to the alcalde, 'let your worship send for the executioner. For this fellow shall tell the truth.' 'It would be better,' replied the alcalde, 'to take him to gaol, and have him tried in due form and put to the torture; and we shall find out who is at the bottom of it all.' This seemed to me to be just; so I sent for the ensign, whom I had not seen for two days, and ordered him to take four soldiers and lead the boy off to gaol, saying I had reason to be afraid. He did so; but, since he was the cause of the evil, he took the boy round by the church of Santo Domingo, and advised him to take refuge there, which he did. He advised the friars not to give him up, or the captain would hang him at once. The monks did as he said, and sent the boy that night to Seville.

Since the cause of my sickness, which was the sublimate, was removed, I began to recover, for God was pleased to preserve me for His own good purposes. I got well and rose from my bed, to the joy of the townspeople; and I resolved to go to Seville with six soldiers. There I made every effort to search for the boy, and I found him easily, and brought him to Osuna, where they desired to catch him and give him an exemplary punishment. The trial took place, and he was put to the question. He confessed that he had done it by order of the ensign, who had offered him great gifts. They wanted to hang him, but found that he was not old enough; so they gave him a hundred lashes in gaol, tied to a post, and cut off the two fingers on each hand with which he had sprinkled the sublimate.

In the confession which I made *in articulo mortis* I had vowed to God, before the confessor, to pardon him who had been the cause of my death. And it was the confessor who had asked me for this promise, for he knew that it was the ensign. The Governor wished to arrest him, but I would not consent. So as soon as the boy had confessed, I sent to summon him, and said, 'Let your worship begone, and God be with you. Do not ask me the reason. But if you have need of anything, tell me, for I will give it you.' He turned as white as death, and went off within the hour, fearing lest I might repent. I learnt afterwards that he had gone off to the Indies; and never more did he appear in Spain. The upshot of it was that I remained for more than two years with my fingers and toes almost crippled, and for ever tingling. Moreover, my strength had gone from me. The doctors said that I did not die because my stomach was used to poison, owing to what they had given me in Rome so short a time before.

The Commissary came. He mustered my company and we marched off in the direction of Sanlúcar, where the armada that was to go to the Philippines was lying in readiness. I was told off to embark on board the galleon *La Concepción*, at the head of three companies which sailed in her.

We left Sanlúcar, shaping our course towards Cadiz, from whence we were to make our departure for the Philippines. But next there came an order from the King that we were not to sail, but to join the Royal Armada and the silver galleons, with all the galleys of Spain, and go to Gibraltar, where, they said, a Dutch fleet was going to touch. Prince Philibert went as Commander-in-Chief.

At the mouth of Cadiz harbour there is a reef fourteen spans below the water, which is called the Diamond, on which many ships have been lost. To crown my ill-luck, I ran upon it, and sank in sight of the whole squadron. Nobody was drowned, for I was aided by all the shallops of the fleet, and the Lord Marquis of Santa Cruz in his Capitana.

The Prince ordered me to be arrested. They brought me to the galleon, on board which I remained during the whole of that expedition. I did not so much as go ashore till I had been given my liberty by the Council of War, seeing that it was not my fault. We cruised up and down the strait from Gibraltar to Cape Espartel (Spartel) with a few ships of the fleet, for more than three months, waiting for the armadas, which we never saw. This was in the January of 1616. In March and April there came an order that that fleet should be split up. This was done, and in particular that portion was detached which was to go to the Philippines, where there was sore need of it. Orders were that the six galleons were to join the Royal Armada, and that the infantry, which was the best in the world, should make its way to Lombardy in charge of Don Carlos de Ibarra, who led it there. The quartermaster of these two thousand five hundred men was Don Pedro Estebán de Ávila, and I remained in Spain with another captain, the order having come in the following terms, in a paragraph of the letter written to the Marquis of Santa Cruz by the King:

'Inasmuch as it is meet that Spain should reinforce the regiments of Lombardy, it is good that Don Pedro Estebán de Ávila, who was to go to the Philippines, should go thither, taking with him the two hundred men whom we thought necessary, with captains expert in navigation, namely, Contreras and Cornejo, who may stay behind to raise men again for this purpose.'

We therefore remained behind, and went to Court, with an order from the Marquis, where we stayed more than six months, till I was ordered to go at once to the Military Board (*Junta de Guerra*) for the Indies at Seville, and orders would reach me on the way as to what I had to do.

I was summoned by the President, Don Fernando Carrillo, who was at the head of that Council, and, having been given five hundred crowns by his order, I took mules that evening for Seville and set out thither.

At Cordoba a packet reached me, in which I was ordered to go and see the paymaster at Seville. I did so on my arrival, and he ordered me to leave for Sanlúcar, where the Duke of Medina would give me instructions. I had audience of His Excellency, and he ordered me in secret to go on to Cadiz with an order for the Governor of that city; and that at nine in the morning two galleys should be there to embark the infantry.

I had audience of the Governor of Cadiz, who gave orders that I should beat up men to reinforce the companies of the fleet which were stationed there. Having assembled them at the house of the King, I was to choose two hundred men and embark them on the two galleys; and they were to be handed over to me with no superior officers – I mean captains, ensigns and sergeants. This was done with the secrecy that was required; otherwise not a single one could have been got on board, for the soldiers of that garrison, and those fleets, are the most arrant ruffians in Andalusia.

I left for Sanlúcar, where the Duke had made ready two galleons of four hundred tons, with their artillery and necessary provisions, in addition to the stores of powder and fuses and lead which they had on board for the fortress which we were going to relieve.

I came to Sanlúcar, and the Duke ordered me to embark the infantry on board the galleons. I did so, placing a hundred on board each, so that they found themselves, as it were, invaded, without knowing what had happened to them.

The other captain came from Court for the other galleon; and we set sail on our expedition, which was to go to the relief of Puerto Rico in the Indies, which was said to be besieged by the Dutch. I remained at Los Pozuelos, as it is called, near La Barra, waiting till the time was ripe. But the soldiers were all pressed men, and were leaving mistresses whom they had had for years. Moreover, they were death's chosen instruments throughout Andalusia. They tried to make fun of me; for when I said, 'Come, gentlemen, turn in, for it is already night,' they answered, 'Are we hens, to go to roost by daylight? Keep calm!' I saw that I was in a tight place, and could not sleep for thinking how I was to get through this voyage; for, apart from fifteen seamen and six artillerymen, I had nobody on my side, for all the hundred soldiers were my enemies. So I set my wits to work, and my eyes fell upon one who seemed the bravest of them, and for whom they had a respect – for even among these fellows there are some whom the other ruffians obey. I called him to me and said, 'Ah, Señor Juan Gomez, come this way.' I took him into the stateroom in the poop and said, 'How long have you been serving the King?' 'It must be five years,' said he. 'At Cadiz and at Larache, from which I ran away, and one cruise with the fleet.' 'Sure now,' I answered, 'I have taken a fancy to you; and sorry I am that I have no ensign to give you.' He was quite set up with himself at this, and said, 'There are others would do it worse than I should.' 'Very well,' said I to him, 'if you would like to be sergeant of this company, go on shore and enlist; and if you have no money to buy a halberd, I will give it you.' 'I still have fifty *pesos*,' said he, 'since your worship does me such honour.' And I may say that there was one man who had offered two hundred pieces of eight if he were allowed to go on shore. I gave him a note for the paymaster, and said, 'Go, your worship, for this is a step towards becoming an ensign. And look you now, I trust you.' He went off in the boat and went on shore and enlisted, and came back at once with his halberd. When the bravos saw him come back as sergeant, they gave up their case for lost. So, carrying out the plan I had resolved upon, I summoned the sergeant to the stateroom and said to him, 'Your worship is now another man. For now that you are an officer, any offence is treason, whereas it is not in a soldier. Tell me, then, by the life of a sergeant, which of these fellow are the most dangerous and the bravest.' Said he, 'Your worship need not ask; for they are a poor lot. Only Calderón and Montañés are anything like decent men.' 'Very well then,' said I. 'At night, when we give the command to turn in, do you stand here with a naked sword.' 'What for, sir? I vow to Christ that a stick is enough.' 'No,' said I, 'for when soldiers forget themselves, they are punished, not with the stick, but with the sword.' Night came; and I said, as was my custom, 'Come, sirs, turn in, for it is high time.' They answered with their accustomed insolence, 'Keep calm!' I was standing near Calderôn, so I raised my sword and gave him such a slash that it laid his brains open. 'Insolent rogues!' I said. 'Go below!' In a twinkling they were all in their mess, like lambs. They came and said to me, 'Sir Captain, Calderôn is dying.' 'Let him confess, and fling him into the sea,' said I, but in other quarters I said he was to be looked after. I at once had Montañés thrown into the bilboes, after which the whole crew remained so submissive that, as for swearing, not a single 'I vow to Christ' was heard during the whole voyage. For if anybody blasphemed I made him stand up for an hour, wearing on his head a great morion that weighed thirty pounds and a breast-plate weighing another thirty.

I sent word to the other captain to do the same. But as soon as they knew what had happened in my galleon they gave up the plan which they had had, which was, on leaving the harbour, to run aground at Arenas Gordas and all take to flight; and to kill me if I tried to stop them.

Chapter xiii

In which is related the Voyage I made to the Indies, and what came to pass there

～

I SET out from port, and sailed for forty-six days without seeing any land but the Canaries. I came to the island of Matalino (Martinique) and watered there. I saw there some wild Indians, for their intercourse with the fleets gives them confidence to descend to the shore. But none of our men landed, for the natives have sometimes captured men; and they eat them. I continued on my course towards the low latitudes and arrived at the Virgenes Gordas (Virgin Islands), which are some other uninhabited islands. My course lay through the passage of Puerto Rico, which is a narrow channel where the English, Dutch and French pirates generally lie. I arrived by night, and went in person to reconnoitre it with a well-armed boat, leaving the galleons outside the channel, which is short and has two very good harbours. I found no ships, so I passed through, finding myself at daybreak almost at the entrance of Puerto Rico, which

ZUCCHERO: SIR WALTER RALEIGH
(National Portrait Gallery)

I entered with flags flying. I was very well received by Don Felipe de Biamonte y Navarra, the Governor of that island.

He told me it was a miracle that I had not encountered Guatarral (Sir Walter Raleigh), an English pirate who was cruising in those waters with five ships, three big ones and two little ones, and harassing him every day. I landed the powder, which he said was needed, and the fuses and lead and a few firearms, with which the good Governor rested content. He asked me to leave him forty soldiers to reinforce the garrison. But never in my life did I find myself in such a fix; for not one of them was willing to stay, and all of them were nearly crying at the thought of stopping there; and they were right, for it would have been to remain in eternal slavery. 'Boys,' I said to them, 'we are bound to leave forty soldiers here. But your worships must pass sentence on yourselves, for I shall not choose anybody, not even the servant I have brought with me. But if the lot falls on him, he must stay.'

I made as many slips of paper as there were soldiers, and among them forty black ones; and, putting them all together into a jar, I shook them up, and then called them up each in turn, according to the roll, saying, 'Let your worship put in your hand, and if you draw a black slip, you must stay behind.' They came and did so; and it was a sight to see how, when they drew a black slip – since they were bound to stay in the end, and saw that it was fair and that they had no choice – they were comforted; and especially when they saw how the lot fell on a servant of mine who served as my barber, which same was the first who had to stay.

In this harbour there were two boats which had to go to Santo Domingo, where are the Law Courts for the Spanish islands, having their President and judges; and this was the first land to be trodden by a Spanish foot. The boats were Spanish. They had to ship cargoes of ox-hides and ginger, which is found there in quantities, and they set forth with me. I arrived at the harbour of Santo Domingo, where I was well received, and began to construct a small fort, which I had orders to set up at the entry of the river.

Two days later, news came that Guatarral (Walter Raleigh) had anchored with his five ships near at hand. I took counsel with the President about going to search for them, and he thought it

meet to do so, though the owners of the ships protested that if these were lost the Government would
have to pay for them. I armed the two which I had
brought from Puerto Rico, and another which had
come from Cape Verde laden with negroes, and I
went forth from the harbour with my ships, as if
we had been merchantmen, on our way to where
they lay. When the enemy saw us, I made as if we
were shaping our course for flight. The enemy
crowded on sail and bore down on us, but we did
not flee, on purpose, and in a short time they were
on us. I turned my prow towards them, ran up my
standards, and we began to let fly at them, and they
at us. They sailed their boats better than we did,
and so when they wished to come close to us, or run
away from us, they could do so; and for this reason
they slipped between my fingers. The fight went
on, and it came to pass that their admiral died of a
shot; and they recognized us for ships of the armada,
and not merchantmen, which had come out to look
for them. Upon this they made off, and I returned
to Santo Domingo, where I finished my fortifica-
tion and left for Cuba, where I made another little
redoubt in four days. And I left ten soldiers there.

I had left fifty soldiers and the three boats at

Santo Domingo, so I now had only one with me, but it was well armed. Santiago de Cuba is a town in the island of Cuba, which is the one in which they built Habana and Bayamo and other towns which I cannot remember.

I left Santiago de Cuba and at the Isle of Pines I found a vessel at anchor. I made short work of her. She was English, one of Guatarral's five. They told me how he had gone away, and disembogued from the channel of the Bahamas; and that his son, who was an admiral, had been killed, with thirteen more persons; and that he had been afraid and gone off to England, taking a few prizes with him. I informed the President of this, and the Governor of Puerto Rico, so that they should not be anxious. This boat had a cargo of Brazil wood and a little sugar, which they had taken on a prize. There were twenty-one Englishmen. I took them to Habana, where they remained till the fleet arrived and bore them away to Spain.

I handed over the rest of my stores and the infantry to Sancho de Alquiza, who was Captain-General of that island and of all those parts; and in the fleet which was returning to Spain I sailed with Don Carlos de Ibarra, who had been General there in the year 1618. I went there and back in the year 1619.

I arrived at Sanlúcar and went on to Seville, where I found Señor Juan Ruiz de Contreras ill. He was equipping a fleet for the Philippines. And the moment I arrived, he told me he had orders from the King that I was to assist him. I did so, and he sent me at once to Borgo, which is where they were getting ready six great galleons and two pataches. I worked in accordance with the orders he had given me, until I brought them down to Sanlúcar out of the careening yards – that is to say, ready caulked. They took on board provisions, the necessary artillery, and the infantry, of which there were more than a thousand men – and fine ones too – besides the crews and artillerymen. The General of this fleet was Don Somebody Zoazola, of the military order of Santiago, who went unwillingly, like all the rest. And this is how they met their end: thirteen days after they had started in fair weather from Cadiz, a tempest caught them, so that they went to destruction six leagues from the place whence they had set forth. It was said, and it was the truth, that it was the Admiral who was the cause of it; for he was no sailor and had never been to sea before. His name was Something-or-another Figueroa, and afterwards, to make things better, they made him Admiral of a fleet, to confirm his first error.

The Capitana and the Admiral went aground at the same spot, and not a splinter of the Capitana was saved, albeit she was a galleon of more than eight hundred tons, and carrying forty pieces of heavy bronze artillery. The General and all the crew were drowned, and not more than four persons were saved. Nearly all the crew of the Admiral were saved, and the galleon did not go to pieces so quickly, for it had gone more deeply aground. The others ran for the straits, and one was lost at Tarifa, another at Gibraltar, and another at Cape Gata. The two pataches were saved. Such was the end of this armada; and in order to salve it — as if it had been my fault — I was sent with two tartans to Tarifa, or the shores near by, to fetch the thirty pieces of bronze artillery which they had taken from the lost galleon. It was known that two galleons from Algiers were standing by, desiring to take the artillery on board; but the people on shore had prevented them. So I arrived with my two tartans and took the guns on board. My orders were, that if the enemy forced me to surrender, in case there was an engagement, I was to sink my ship with all the artillery – lest they might make use of it – and order the other tartan to do the same. I came along hugging the shore, with the enemy to seaward, so that they could do me no harm, and I carried off the artillery in safety.

A few days later news was brought to Cadiz that La Mámora (Mehedia) was besieged by sea and by land, and that thirty thousand Moors on the land side had made three attacks on it; while out at sea there were twenty-eight galleons of war, both Turkish and Dutch, to hinder the arrival of reinforcements.

The Duke of Medina Sidonia commanded that reinforcements should at once be provided, and Señor Don Fadrique de Toledo immediately got ready the galleons of his fleet. But he had not time to make the voyage, so two tartans were got ready, with powder, fuses and shot, all of which they were short of; for they had used up the very ropes with which they drew water from the wells or reservoirs, and those which held up the cots, which are the beds in which the soldiers sleep. I saw that these tartans had got to be sent; but when they ordered the captains of the garrison to choose some of the toughest old campaigners, nobody would come forward. So I came to the Duke and said, 'Sir, I beseech Your Excellency to entrust this expedition to me; and for this favour, you may brand my face with an S and a nail, as if I were a slave.' (Esse (S) – clavo = slave.) He thought well of this, and commanded me to go. When the captains of the garrison saw that it had been entrusted to me, they went to the Duke and said that it should have been given to one of them – since they were under His Excellency's command – and not to me, for I was not under his command, but was there to fit out the fleet for the Philippines. I heard of this, and said in public that it had been given to me at my own request, and not till after they had been sent word to get ready some men from their companies. But since none of them had asked for it, I had. That I was a captain of infantry and senior to any of them. And that if anybody was minded otherwise, I was ready to meet him at Santa Catalina in single combat. As I was on my way to the appointed place, an adjutant came on behalf of the Duke, who had sent for me. I turned back, and he ordered me to obtain leave from Señor Juan Ruiz de Contreras, for I was under his orders. When I had got it, he gave me instructions as to what I was to do, and, in particular, that with good luck and God's help, I was to relieve the garrison or let myself be cut in pieces.

Chapter xiv

How I relieved the Forces at La Mámora and other Happenings

～

I SET sail, and so calculated my time – for it is forty-two leagues away – that at daybreak I found myself in the midst of the twenty-eight ships. I timed it so well that everything went off as I had planned. I judged that the enemy's fleet must be anchored at least a league out at sea, to be out of range of the artillery, and because the bar is so rough and sets up such a surge, that the breakers begin a mile out, as I have mentioned. But if I was in the midst of them by daybreak, I could get across the bar, for the waves as they broke would carry me over. So that if any of the ships determined to follow me, they would have to enter the river in my wake, or cut across to the shore. However, it all went off as I have described, for by the time they had seen me, there was nothing to be done, save to fire a few shots at me from their muskets and cannon. But there were not many of them, for in such a short time they could not hurt me.

I entered like the dove from the ark. They embraced me a thousand times, and so did good old Lechuga, the Governor, who had defended it like the brave man he was.

They began to unload the munitions, and the ships started weighing anchor, for they thought the Royal Armada would soon be upon them. And they were right, for it was there by the evening of next day. I went to dine with the Governor; but while I was so doing the drums beat to arms. When we inquired what was afoot they said that it was six bravos (*matasiete*) coming on an errand of peace. Orders were given to admit them, and take them to the house of a Jew there who acts as interpreter; for it was the custom for them to go there. They gave them food to eat and tobacco to smoke; and so I found them. These bravos are so called because they are gentlemen, and indeed they looked it, for I saw they had very nice embroidered sword-belts, and very nice buskins, and fine robes and Fez caps, unlike the costume of the Moors of those parts. Lechuga, the quartermaster, gave orders that all the powder and fuses should be fetched up, and carried past the house where the Moors were, and likewise the soldiers I had brought with me; for they had good clothing, but those who were there were going naked.

We went to the house where the Moors were, and they rose and exchanged salutes with us. They sat down again and drank our healths, and we drank too; and they are as good drinkers as the porters of Madrid. The munitions started going by, and they had a good look at them, and at the soldiers too.

They said they had come to take leave of the Governor, because seven thousand of those bravos were going away that evening, and all the rest that night. They wished to have his friendship, and would send him five hundred sheep and thirty cows for sale, if he would buy them. He said that he would. He gave them a lot of tobacco, which is the greatest treat you can give them. They could not live if it were not for La Mámora; for they bring all that they steal and sell it there, as well as what they do not steal. They give you a sheep as big as an ox for four reals, and a cow for sixteen, and a bushel and a half of wheat for three, and a fowl for half a real. Upon this they departed, and I prepared to depart too. This La Mámora is a river, which has at its mouth the aforesaid bar; but great ships can enter into it; and if the enemy held it, they could do great damage to Spain; for it is not more than forty-two leagues from Cadiz. And as our fleets sail from and return to that port, or Sanlúcar, the Moors might easily do us great damage by capturing our ships, and get back home within the day, without having to make the long voyage to Algiers or Tunis; not to speak of the risks they take in going through the Strait of Gibraltar. This river goes up to Tlemçen, thirty leagues inland, and is navigable throughout, and, thanks to the advantage of cheap victuals, they can fit out a fleet very well there. It was for this reason that the Dutch were so greedy to get it.

To show the harm they could do us in this way because it is so navigable, and, as I have said, because great galleons can sail up it: three leagues away, on the same coast, there is a place which they call Sallee, with a very good fortress. The Andalusian Moriscoes are the masters of it; and there is a little creek which will not admit any but small boats like tartans and pataches. Yet with these they harass the coast of Spain; and not a year passes but more than five hundred slaves enter Sallee, taken from ships near to our coasts, coming from the Indies and the Azores and Canaries, and from Brazil and Pernambuco. They take a prize, and are home again in a night, and they do this on the coast of Portugal by day and by night. People will say that I am going outside the story of my life and am meddling with history; but on my faith, I am well able to do so.

That night I went out from the bar of La Mámora and by daybreak was at Cadiz; I mean, I entered the port before midday. I went to Conil, where the Duke was staying. He invited me to dine, and at dessert he read the letter of credit which I bore from the Governor to the King. He was glad to see it, and told me to lose no time in going to Madrid. He gave me a letter for the King and an honourable testimonial, which I value highly, with a hundred doubloons in a purse. For the servants said it was the greatest exploit he had achieved in his life. I went to the Puerto de Santa Maria, where the purveyor of the frontiers gave me a hundred and fifty crowns for post-horses, so that in three and a half days I dismounted in Madrid. So within nine days I had entered Madrid, left Spain and gone to Barbary, afterwards returning from Barbary to Spain and from thence to Court, which is a hundred and eight land leagues from Cadiz. I dismounted at the

VELAZQUEZ: YOUTHFUL PORTRAIT OF PHILIP IV OF SPAIN
(Prado)

Palace and went up without my cloak to the King's apartments. There came forward Señor Don Baltasar de Zúñiga – God rest his soul! – and I gave him a report of it all. I next entered with His Excellency into the King's presence, and on bended knee handed him the two letters, the letter of credit and the letter from the Duke. He gave them to Señor Don Baltasar. The King began to question me about the affair of La Mámora, for, said Señor Don Baltasar, 'Lechuga refers us to him in his letter.' I gave all the information His Majesty required, so much so, that he took hold of the cord hanging from my habit and twirled it round while he asked questions and I replied. Shortly afterwards Señor Don Baltasar said, 'Go and rest, for you must be tired from your journey.' I went down through the courts, and there was the porter of the Council of State waiting for me; for it was sitting that day. He took me in, and their lordships were all standing up. They questioned me as to how things were going. I gave my report, and they were well pleased. Upon which I left, and went off on my post-horses to the house of an uncle whom I have at that Court, the head of the posts of Portugal. I rested, for I had need of it,

On the morrow there came a halberdier to my lodging to summon me in the name of Señor Don Baltasar. I went with great content, and although he was surrounded by many people wishing to speak with him, they made way for me. He seated himself in a chair, and told me to sit down in another, and when he asked me what positions I had held, for His Majesty desired to show me favour, I said that I had been a captain in the Spanish infantry and was at present engaged in refitting the Philippine fleet, and salving the remains of it; and that my pay had been at the rate of fifty crowns a month for more than two years past.

He asked what were my inclinations, and what I had an eye to. 'Sir,' said I, 'I do not plume myself upon my record. The Council has mentioned my name for a place as admiral of a fleet.' He said, 'By Jesus, Sir Captain, it shall be given you on the spot, with a nice little sum for your expenses.' I kissed his hand for this, and he told me to apply to the secretary, Juan de Ynsástigui, who would give me my commission. I went off to my house with great content, and on the morrow I went in to find Ynsástigui in his office, and found with him Señor Don Baltasar, who said to me, 'How goes it? Let your worship take this commission and this draft, and have patience, for His Majesty can do no more for you at present as regards maravedis.' I said, 'Sir, I need no money if it is so scarce. It is honour that I seek, not wealth'; and I returned him the draft. But he would not let me leave it, though he thought highly of my liberality, and told me so. The draft was for three hundred ducats in solid silver, and the other letter a royal order for Don Fernando Carrillo, President of the Indies.

I took it to the President, and he received it with his heretic's face – for he had no other – and dismissed me shortly; saying that His Majesty's orders would be executed all in good time.

One or two months went by, and he did not propose me for a place. I applied to Señor Don Baltasar, and he gave me a letter, in which he ordered them not to wait for a meeting of the Council, for the King desired to show me favour. I presented the note; but the worthy heretic must have pledged his word to somebody else, for he filled up the place and left me out of it. I heard about it at once, and, without more delay, I went to seek audience of the King – for at that time whosoever desired audience of him would wait in the

corridors. 'Sir,' I said, 'I have served Your Majesty
for twenty-five years in many places, as is shown in
this memorial, and by my last service in relieving
the garrison at La Mámora, Your Majesty honoured
me with a decree that I should be given the position
of admiral of a fleet; for in view of my services I
have been proposed as such on other occasions.
But now, though Your Majesty has ordered it to be
given me, the President has not yet appointed me.'
He took my memorial, snatching it from my hands,
and, turning his back to us, he went off, leaving us
all confounded; for he was newly come to the throne.
I went off to Señor Don Baltasar for consolation
and to lay my complaint before him as my chief. I
was there, awaiting the appointed time, when the
President arrived with the face I have described,
for he was swallowing a bitter pill, or had been sent
one from a high quarter. As he went in, I entered
with him, though the porter, or a gentleman who
was there, would have stopped me. 'Let me pass,
your worship,' said I, 'for I come on the same business as the Lord President.' I went in, and there
was Señor Don Baltasar with the Count of Monterey, afterwards my master, and a Dominican friar,
the son of the Count of Benavente, and Señor Don

Baltasar standing in the middle of the room with the President. I went up to them and said, 'I entreat Your Excellency to ask my Lord President if he is satisfied with me personally.' He threw out his hands, and answered, 'Sir, you are a most honourable soldier; and we sent you to Puerto Rico, where you did very well.' On this I said to him, 'Then if I am so honourable, why did Your Lordship not appoint me, when the King had given the order, and His Excellency had sent you a further letter?' 'Another time, sir,' said he. 'The matter is already settled.' 'Do not believe it, Your Excellency,' I said thereupon, 'for he is deceiving you as he deceived me.' Then he shouted in a loud voice, 'Fellow, the matter is settled.' 'Look now, Your Excellency,' replied Señor Don Baltasar, 'the King desires to bestow a favour upon the captain.' He could not speak, he was so choked with rage; and he left the room. And before he reached the street he fell senseless. They laid him in his carriage for dead, and bandaged his arms and legs tightly to make him come to himself. God restored him to his senses, and he confessed and died. God pardon him the harm he did me! He lost his life and I my place as admiral. For Señor Don Baltasar, who was my chief, said it was not

[215]

right that I should receive any favour, for I had killed a minister as if I had shot him with an arquebus. Was it not rather the fault of a certain letter which he received from high quarters, which, I heard, was what gave him his death-blow?

Upon this I withdrew from the Palace, and ceased to go there any more. More than six months had gone by when, one day, as I was thinking of nothing, a halberdier came to fetch me on behalf of his lordship the Count of Olivares. I went to him, anxious to know what he wanted with me. As I went into the room where he was, the first thing he said to me was, 'Sir Captain Contreras, make no complaints, though well I know that you have cause to do so. The King has resolved to form an armada to guard the Strait of Gibraltar, and I am its Captain-General; and the Navy Board (*Junta de Armadas*) has appointed sixteen captains drawn from different parts, practised men with experience. Of the two chosen from those who are at this Court, one is Quartermaster Don Pedro Osorio, and your worship is the other. I hope you value this.' I thanked His Excellency for the favour which he was conferring on me, and said to him, 'Sir, I find myself with fifty crowns' pay and have twice been captain. It is not meet that I should once again take a company, and give up the fifty crowns which I draw in the fleet.' 'There is no need to discuss this,' he said to me, 'for the question of raising your pay is my affair.' On which I said, 'Then will Your Excellency allow me to raise my company here at Court?' He said it had never been done; but that, to satisfy me, he would speak about it to His Majesty. He obtained permission for both the Quartermaster and me to raise our companies there; and we were the first captains to enrol men and fly our flags while the Court was in residence.

Chapter xv

How I raised another Company of Infantry in
Madrid at Antón Martín, and other Happenings

~

I SET up my flag at Antón Martín in Madrid, and
in twenty-seven days I enrolled three hundred
and twelve soldiers and marched forth before the
eyes of the whole Court, with them drawn up in
file and I at the head of them. This was a consolation to my good mother for all the griefs which my
vicissitudes in this world have caused her.

Two days after I left the Court, the report was
spread about that I had been murdered at Getafé,
and they sorrowed in Madrid as if I had been a
great lord; and as to this I call to witness whosoever
was present there. They say that it was the Marquis
of Barcarrota who said it on the pelota-ground, and
this and no other was its origin; on which account
Señor Don Francisco de Contreras, President of
Castille, sent post-haste to learn the truth, in order
to avenge the deed if it had happened as they
said. I sent word that I was well, and they were

glad at Court; so important it is to be well beloved.

From this false death, ascribed to me by certain good people, I gained more than five hundred Masses at the Buen Suceso. I heard that offerings were made for saying more than three hundred. I heard it afterwards from the controller of the hospital, when he was soliciting a place; and his name was Don Diego de Cordoba. I went on to Cadiz with my company, and entered it with more than three hundred soldiers. We embarked, and set out for the Strait, where we were stationed. This armada was commanded by Don Juan Fajardo, who was its Captain-General. I sailed on the Admiral of Naples; and in this squadron there were six splendid ships, of which Francisco de Ribera was Captain-General; and the whole armada was made illustrious by his ships and his valour. They belonged to those which the Lord Duke of Osuna had at Naples; and would to God that the good Ribera had been Captain-General of all this armada, for His Majesty would have been served very differently, and we should have won glory. The whole armada consisted of twenty-two great galleons and three pataches. A few of us were told off to sail from Gibraltar, and go out to meet some Turkish ships, which were passing through the Straits and coasting along the shores of Africa; though it is not more than three leagues' distance across this strait from Spain to Barbary. In this expedition, we took a few prizes.

After many days, on OCTOBER 6, 1624, we met the fleet of Holland, which was of eighty-two sail, though not all were warships. We went out to meet them beyond Malaga, fifteen leagues out at sea. All I know is that Ribera's Capitana and my galleon, which was the Admiral, came into action with the enemy at four o'clock in the afternoon; that is, Ribera's galleon, Don Juan Fajardo's Capitana, and the Admiral, in which I was sailing. I cannot tell what happened, except that the enemy went off laughing at us. But had it not been that Ribera's Capitana received a cannon-shot below the water-line, so that they had to lower a boat and stop it, God knows how things would have gone with the enemy. The cannon-shot which he received was from no Christian ball, neither did it come from the enemy's ships. But to pass on: night fell, and that night they went off and passed through the Straits, with none to molest them, which they had never dreamt of doing. For they would readily have purchased this advantage by the loss of a quarter of their ships, as we were afterwards told. We returned to Gibraltar, and Don Juan Fajardo stayed behind there, while we went off with Ribera in search of the silver galleons, which we met and brought back to Sanlúcar, besides the ships which we took from the Turks on the way, and a prize of sugar which they had with them.

We returned to our winter quarters at Gibraltar, and I fell ill. I was given twenty days' leave to go and spend my convalescence at Seville.[1] But because I outstayed it, Don Juan Fajardo disposed of my company. I went to Court and laid a complaint, and His Majesty granted me the favour of a command over five hundred infantry, who were to go and serve in four companies in the galleys of Genoa. I raised the infantry. But as I was on the point of marching away, I was given orders to go with it to Lisbon and embark in an armada which had been built to oppose that of England, under the command of Tomás de Larraspur.

We waited at Cascães and Belén for more than two months, for news had come that the English

[1] See the memorial drawn up by Contreras on this occasion in Appendix III, which explains the General's action more fully.

fleet was going to no other place than Lisbon, whither it had been summoned by the Jews. But when they saw that we were ready, they turned towards Cadiz. Although this was known, we received orders not to leave that harbour, where we remained until we knew that the armada had withdrawn to England.

The Marquis of Hinojosa, who held the position of Commander-in-Chief by sea and land, was beginning to disband the army, and I, with the men of my troop, was included in this, for we had gone back to Madrid, to await the order to depart to our galleys. But they had grown cold about this plan because they said there was war in Lombardy; and this would not have been, but that the Genoese are powerful. And, although the Duke of Tarsis (Tursi) gave his aid, by having his galleys manned by Spaniards, he could not succeed, for the time being, in having the plan carried into effect. So we remained as poor suitors at Court; though I did not come off badly. For Lope de Vega, to whom I had never spoken in my life, carried me off to his house, saying, 'Sir Captain, with men like your worship one would share one's cloak.' He kept me as his companion for more than eight months, giving me

F. LOPE FELIX DE VEGA CARPIO
del habito de S. Juan, Poeta Lirico, Epico, y Dra-
matico de maravillosa fecundidad. Nació en
Madrid en 1562; falleció en 1635.

LOPE DE VEGA WEARING THE HABIT OF THE ORDER OF ST. JOHN OF
JERUSALEM
(British Museum, Print Room)

my dinner and supper; and he even gave me clothes. May God requite him! And he was not content with this, but must needs dedicate to me, in part twenty of his works, a comedy called *The King without a Kingdom*, copied from the evidence which was brought against me about the Moriscoes.[1]

It seemed to me shameful to stay at Court, especially as I had nothing to live upon; for soldiers are not in their place there, even if they have means. So I took steps to go to Malta, and see how the affairs of my Order stood, and when it would help me to find something to eat. I petitioned the Council to grant me pay for Sicily, which is near Malta; and they gave me thirty crowns for maintenance, five more than they give captains now. And so I went my way to Barcelona, and from thence set sail for Genoa and Naples and Sicily. I presented my draft, my pay was given me, and a month later, when I desired to go on leave to Malta, the Duke of Albuquerque, the Viceroy of that kingdom, conferred on me the honour of the governorship of Pantanalea (Pantellaria), an island which is almost in Barbary. It includes lands and a fortress, with a

[1] See Appendix I, Lope de Vega's dedication to Contreras of *El Rey sin Reino*.

hundred and twenty Spanish soldiers. I passed through Malta on my way there, and found I had not served or been in residence for the term of years which would have qualified me to hold a commandery. Besides which, the commanderies to be had by those with the rank of sergeant are few and small, and the best of them is not worth six hundred ducats.

I held this governorship for sixteen months, and had a few slight affrays with those who come there to get meat and water. I also busied myself about the church, in which was held the confraternity of Our Lady of the Rosary, which was thatched with reeds and straw like a wine-shop. I sent to Sicily for wood, and for a painter and paints. I rebuilt this church, roofing it with good planks and beams. I made six arches of stone, a tribune and a sacristy. I painted the whole church, the roof and the choir, with the four evangelists upon the walls, and I had the altar of Our Lady painted upon wooden slabs. And then I made an arch with God the Father over it; and in the arch were the fifteen mysteries, each mystery being depicted.

I endowed it with a perpetual income for the following purpose: that every year during the last three days of Carnival, on the last Thursday before Lent, there should be a sung Mass, with deacon and subdeacon, and a catafalque hung with black cloths and candles; besides a dozen low Masses, and, at vespers, the office for the dead with catafalque and candles; all this for the souls in purgatory. Item, I left a sum of money, so that, when they learn of my decease, they may be obliged to say two hundred Masses for my soul. Besides this, I left a sum for cleaning the paintings, and whitewashing the church every two years. And further, I left a low Mass for my soul every month, in the finest and most ornate style the island could afford.

So the church was adorned to the best of my ability; on which I asked leave of the Lord Duke of Albuquerque to go to Rome with him. He gave it me unwillingly for four months. I came to Palermo, and there embarked for Naples, and from thence came to Rome.

I took steps to obtain a brief, to exempt me from the term of service and residence which I was obliged to spend in the Order so as to have a commandery. But when I proposed this to His Holiness, he would not grant it, upon which I resolved to speak with him. He received me in audience, and

I gave him an account of my services, and said that the treasure of the church was for men like me, who had had their fill of serving in defence of the Catholic faith. Upon which His Holiness, in consideration of my labours and their Christian merit, not only granted me a facultative brief, but also made it gratuitous. Moreover, he gave me another, in which the Order is commanded to admit me to the rank of knight in consideration of my services, enjoying due seniority, and that I should be eligible for all the commanderies and dignities enjoyed by the knights of justice. Moreover, he granted me in perpetuity a privileged altar for the island of Pantanalea, in my church, no more than three Masses being necessary to obtain the plenary indulgence; and this was granted to the altar for seven years; with which I rested content. But the best part of it was still undone, namely, to despatch these affairs with Monsignori the ministers; for, in their opinion, these graces were many, and such as had never before been seen, which is the truth; so they hedged them about with a thousand saving clauses. But all this was straightened out by the Count of Monterey, my master, and my lady the Countess, his wife, by messages and letters which they wrote to the ministers; for it would have been impossible to obtain all this had it not been for Their Excellencies. Their Excellencies were at that time Ambassadors extraordinary in Rome; and when I had despatched my business I desired to go to Malta and Palermo, where my pay was waiting for me. But when I asked leave of His Excellency, he ordered me, for certain causes which arose, not to leave Rome. I did not do so, and the Count appreciated it, and ordered his treasurer that I should be given thirty crowns a month, which was done with great promptitude.

I asked leave of His Excellency, after six months were past, in order that I might present my briefs. He gave me leave for two months, within which I was to return. I left Rome, and went to Naples and Sicily, and from thence to Malta, where I presented the briefs, with letters from His Excellency. They were instantly obeyed, and they armed me as knight with all the necessary ceremonies, and gave me a Bull which I esteem more highly than if I had been born of the Infante Carlos. In it is said how, for my notable deeds and exploits, they arm me knight, enjoying all the commanderies and dignities of the Order which are enjoyed by the knights of justice.

That day there we feasted high at a great banquet. I left Malta to return to Rome, and arrived in a short time; for in going and coming, doing my business and returning to Rome, I was less than thirty-four days, though the distance came to almost three hundred leagues.

I came to Rome, and kissed the hand of the Count my master, and my lady the Countess. They were glad of my despatch and of my quick return.

Eight days after my arrival at Rome, the Count my master ordered me to go with two of his country coaches, which had six horses each, and fetch the lord Cardinals Sandoval and Espínola (Spinola) and Albornoz, who were coming from Spain, and were to land at the harbour of Palo, twenty miles from Rome. He likewise ordered me to invite them in his name to come and lodge in his house, where he had had sumptuous quarters prepared for them.

I arrived at Palo, where Their Eminences were at the castle. I discharged my mission. They appreciated it greatly, but replied that they could not think of entering Rome, for it was the bad season, but would go to some other place near Rome. When they had come to this decision, I entreated them to consider well, and put the service of the

King first. So they took the risk of losing their health, and, two hours before nightfall, gave orders to get the coaches ready; and there were as many as seventeen country coaches.

The three lord Cardinals took their places in the coach of the Count my master, and their chamberlains and I in the other. They began to urge on the horses, one and all, to save them from a sunstroke. I made such good haste that I entered Rome at dawn, with none but the two coaches of the Count my master; and none of the seventeen could follow me. In these I brought them to the house very early on St. Peter's Day, when the horse is presented to the Pope.

They were lodged in the house of the Count my master, each one in his apartments, in such pomp and profusion as can be imagined, with their chamberlains and other servants.

They stayed there till they took houses, which must have been a month; and there they were visited by all the College of Cardinals, and entertained by the Count my master. And I returned to my inn, where I remain, and will remain, until His Excellency shall give me further orders; for I desire nothing but to serve him. One thing I will tell, for it was a miracle. These lords entered Rome on St. Peter's Day, when the bad season is at its height. But of all the households which they brought with them – and there were more than three hundred persons – nobody died; and Their Eminences had not so much as a headache. So I say it is nonsense about the bad season. It is true I told them at Palo that they must protect themselves from the sun, and on entering Rome must keep quiet, for in this way there would be no changes of climate. These are the events which have happened up to to-day, which is the 11th of OCTOBER, 1630. But if I had tried to write down all the details, it would weary those who might read it. Besides, it is certain I have forgotten many things; for in eleven days one cannot give an abstract of one's memories, and the deeds and happenings of thirty-three years. Here it is, quite simple and without ornament, as God made it and as best I could manage, without rhetoric or fine style, but just as it happened in very deed and truth. Christ be praised!

Chapter xvi

Arrival of the Marquis of Cadreyta at Rome.
Eruption of Vesuvius. My stay at the Casales
of Capua. My Governorship of the City of
Aquila

ॐ

IT next came to pass that the Count my master
resolved to entertain the Lord Marquis of Cadreyta, who was going as Ambassador Ordinary to
Germany, and was passing through Rome as
Ambassador of the Most Serene the Queen of
Hungary. The Count my master ordered me to
go and receive him on his journey, and offer him
his house. But since he had not brought letters from
the Queen in the form which is necessary if the Pope
is to receive him as Ambassador, he had to be taken
to Frascati, a great pleasure-house, where he was
entertained till the Queen wrote again. He then
entered Rome and came to stay in the house of the
Count my master, where he was entertained and
served. And after he had kissed the Pope's foot and
received his visit, and his lordship had returned it,
he left for Ancona, where he met the Queen and

set sail for the Imperial Court, to discharge and carry out his embassy. And his mission to Rome was very brilliant and magnificent, worthy of such a lord.

Next, after a few days, the Count my master sent me to beg a galley from her ladyship the Countess of Tarsis (Tursi), for the secretary Juan Pablo Boneti and me to depart in and perform certain business at Madrid. The galley came. We embarked on it and came to Barcelona, and from thence I had orders to ride post-haste, for the business was pressing. I did so, and thus the Count my master had his wish, for I arrived speedily.

I stayed in Madrid more than two months (1630), where I rejoiced to see the fine comedies of the Phœnix of Spain, Lope de Vega, who is so eminent in all things, and has given us such an example in his books, that there is nobody who may not be a poet and write comedies. For the existence of this man alone would have been an honour to Spain, and the wonder of other nations.

From Madrid I had orders to depart for Naples, where the Count my master was Viceroy; and when I arrived he told me to take a company of Spanish infantry. I told him that I had already done so four times. He insisted, and I took it, so that I

became his bodyguard. Two months later, he sent me to garrison the city of Nola. And as I was there quiet one morning, on Tuesday the 16th of DECEMBER, there appeared at dawn a great plume of smoke over the mountain of Soma, which others call Vesuvius; and, as day broke, the sun began to be darkened, and it thundered and rained ashes. I would have you know that Nola is almost directly under the mountain, four miles or less away. The people began to be afraid, seeing that day had become night, and that it was raining ashes; so they began to leave the place. And that night was so terrible, that I think the Day of Judgment could appear no otherwise. For besides ashes, it was raining earth and fiery stones, like the slag which the smiths take out of the forges, some as big as one's hand, some larger and some smaller. Besides all this, there was a constant trembling of the earth, so that on that night thirty-seven houses fell; and one heard the cypresses and orange trees rent asunder as if cleft by an axe of iron. Everyone was crying 'Misericordia,' so that it was terrible to hear. On Wednesday there was hardly any light, so that we had to have the lamps lit. I went forth with a squadron of soldiers, and fetched seven loads of

[233]

flour, and told them to bake bread, with which we ministered to many who had gone outside the place, so as not to be under a roof. There were in this place two convents of nuns, who would not leave their houses, though the Vicar gave them a licence to do so before he left. These convents collapsed; but it did no injury to anyone, for they were in the body of the church, praying to God.

The soldiers of my company almost mutinied against me; and this was how it happened: they took counsel together, saying that they would come in a body and force me to leave the place, for the fire was drawing near. I found them all together in a street, coming for the aforesaid purpose; and when I saw them I said to them, 'Whither away, gentlemen?' And one replied, 'Sir . . .' but before he could say anything, I answered, 'Gentlemen, let him who will go take himself off; but I do not mean to leave here till my calves are scorched. And when I reach that pass, well, the flag weighs but little, and I will carry it myself.' To this nobody could find any answer. We spent that day, at times in the darkness of night, at times with a gleam of daylight. The misery was such as cannot be told, or even known. For to see the few people who had

THE COUNT OF MONTEREY, VICEROY OF NAPLES
(British Museum, Print Room)

stayed, the women all dishevelled and the little children not knowing which way to turn, waiting for the real night to come; and how here two houses would fall, there another would be on fire – imagine it! And by whatever way one tried to get out, it was impossible, for one was deluged in the ashes and earth which fell on the Thursday morning. And the element of water was at work, though the fire never ceased, nor did the rain of ashes and earth; for there arose such a torrent on the mountain that the sound of it alone struck terror. One branch of it was travelling in the direction of Nola; so I took thirty shovels, and made a trench, so that it turned aside into another direction and struck two little villages, which it swept away like ants, with all the cattle and larger beasts, which could not escape. So I thought to myself that if I had gone off when the soldiers came and begged me to go, the place would have been inundated.

On the Friday, God willed that rain should fall from heaven, mingled with earth and ashes, which made a cement so strong that it was impossible to cut it, even with picks and hoes. This gave me a little consolation, for if the fire pressed us, we might find a way out.

On Saturday almost all the barracks collapsed
in which the company was quartered. But this in-
jured nobody, for the soldiers would rather be in
the open, in the rain and ashes, than in the barracks
or the church, which was damaged, and swayed
with the recurrent shocks, like water with which
one rinses one's mouth.

On Sunday came an order from the Count, who
thought all was lost, since they had been unable
to get through to us. He commanded me to leave
and go to Capua; and though I grieved indeed at
leaving those nuns, who, when they saw me leave,
would be sure to lose heart, I was bound to take
advantage of the order, lest I might be blamed
in case of any mishap. I set out with what I had
on me, for even if I had wished to take my chest,
there was nothing to take it in. We arrived at
Capua, and it was pitiful to see us; so disfigured were
we, that we looked like nothing so much as work-
men from hell. Most of us were barefoot, with our
clothes, and even our bodies, half burnt. We stayed
here for a week to recover, and feasted jovially at
Christmas, though Vesuvius was still vomiting fire.

At the end of a week, the Count sent me a warrant
to quarter my men in the Casales of Capua. I did

so, and there we made good a little of what we had
lost. For my part, they brought me from Nola two
chests of clothing, for all the rest of my houseful
of gear was lost. I was lucky not to have lost the
chests as well.

In the Casales there is a custom that is very hard
on the poor; and it is as follows: the rich, who are
able to have soldiers quartered on them, make one
of their sons take the minor orders of priesthood.
They then transfer to him all their property, so that
they cannot afford to take in soldiers. And the
Archbishop takes their part, because they provide
for him. I reported this swindling to the Bishop,
but he answered that it was fair. I was indignant;
so, taking the soldiers out of the houses of the poor,
I transferred them to those of these rich people. I
would ask, 'Which is the apartment of him who
is in orders?' And they would say, 'This one.' 'Let
it be kept,' I would say, 'with the same respect as
Sunday. But as to these others, who sleeps in them?'
'Sir, the father, the mother, the sisters and brothers.'
And I would quarter three or four soldiers on them.
They complained to the Archbishop; and he wrote
telling me to beware, for I was excommunicated. I
laughed at that; so one of those wild clerics, for so

they call them in that realm, because they have taken only minor orders – and many of them are married – mounted his mare to go and complain to the Archbishop. One of the soldiers gave a jerk to his bridle, saying he was to wait until they had told me. The mare was as used to the bit as her master was to Latin; so she reared and threw him, which did not do him much good.

In this wretched plight he went off to lodge his complaint. On which the Bishop sent to tell me that I was excommunicated, in virtue of the rubric *Quisquis pariente del diablo.* I answered that he must mind what he was doing, for the rubric *Quisquis* meant nothing to me, neither was I a relation of the devil, nor were there any such among my forbears. But let him be careful, for if I made up my mind to being excommunicate, nobody would be safe from me nearer than the fifth sphere. For to that intent had God given me ten fingers on my two hands, and five hundred Spaniards. He took my letter and made no answer, except to send word to the Casales that they should exert themselves and persuade the Viceroy to remove me from thence; and that he would do the same, for there was nothing else to be done. They set to work to press for my removal; but in the meantime I made the rich pay for it, and no poor man suffered. And the time was not so short but it lasted for more than forty days.

When this time was past, the Viceroy sent me to the city of Aquila, one of the greatest in the realm, where they had treated their bishop disrespectfully, and even tried to kill him. My orders were to punish the culprits. I left the Casales on FEBRUARY 9, and crossed the Five Mile Plain, as it is called, where snow was lying to the depth of half a pike. I had a nice time of it on that plain with the soldiers!

This city is so rebellious because it is on the very outskirts of the Romagna, where the King is hardly recognized. I took with me a hundred and fifty Spaniards, of the kind who would as soon take a penny as a halfpenny, and entered the city in skirmishing order with my men in grey. I bore the titles of Governor and Military Governor. I began to make arrests, and they started running away. I quartered my men in grey in the houses of the culprits, where they managed to make themselves comfortable. And I issued a proclamation that nobody was to enter or leave the city bearing firearms – for it was as much their habit to carry them as to wear hats. They obeyed me on the spot, which everyone said was a miracle. But one day there came to the Naples gate six servants of the Viceroy of the province, who was the Count of Chiaramonte, with their muskets and small pistols. They wore their hair very long, like Nazarenes, which is the mark here of bandits or highwaymen – which amounts to the same thing. They were told they could not enter without an order from the Governor and Military Governor. They replied that they did not recognize the Military Governor. And since, of the four soldiers who were at the gate, two had gone to their dinner, they entered, and went swaggering round the market-place in defiance of everybody, as they had always done. I heard of this, so I sent word to shut the gates of the city; and I went out to look for them with eight soldiers. I found them looking as if they had done nothing at all; but when I tried to seize them they began to use their arms, and they had very good ones. But it availed them little, for I closed with them as is the way in the Romagna, and arrested them, though they wounded one of my soldiers.

As soon as they were taken, I at once tried them, giving two hours' grace to each of them. But when

these two hours had expired, I condemned them
to have their Nazarene hair cut and wear it round
their necks; and having hoisted each one on to his
ass, as is the custom in my country, I had each of
them given two hundred lashes, which was done
in the most elegant fashion, though the executioner
was a novice at this sort of justice, which was new
to him, and also to the city. On dismounting from
their asses, they were treated with salt and vinegar,
as is done in the galleys; and next day I sent them
off to the galleys of Naples for six years each, to
await employment about the person of the captain
to whom they were entrusted.

This act of justice seemed impossible to the Lord
Viceroy or President of the province; so when he
had made sure that it had happened, he wrote asking
me by what authority I had done it. I answered,
in virtue of my authority as Military Governor. I
told him to argue it out with the Count of Monterey, who had sent me my commission. So upon
this he determined to come and arrest me at Aquila;
to which end he collected three hundred horsemen
and a few foot. I heard of this, and wrote to him
that his lordship should be careful, or he would
have the whole countryside in rebellion; and it was

already partly so, because I had come to mete out punishment. And since he was a Minister of the King, he should not attempt anything of the sort without reporting it to the Count as Viceroy of the kingdom; who, if I had done wrong, would punish me. He took no notice of this, but tried to follow out his intention. Having spies, I saw that he was in earnest; so I proceeded to choose a hundred from among the hundred and fifty Spaniards whom I had with me, with powder, fuses and bullets. I put on my pistols, mounted a spirited horse which I had, and took a thousand crowns about my person as caution-money. I went out to wait for him at a certain place, from which I wrote him a letter, saying that, since he took so little trouble in the service of the King, he had better go his way and take a good horse, for if I caught him, I swore to Christ that I should have him thrashed like the others. And I should have done it as soon as talk about it, for I was sure that I could subdue his men, who were all riff-raff. And when I had done as I have said, I should go off to Rome and Milan and Flanders, so that there would be an end of it all. Besides, from where I was, I could reach the States of the Church in six hours.

He resolved to take my letter and send it to the Viceroy, the Count of Monterey; and he returned to his house or estate, and I to mine.

On the morrow I received warning that there was a knight going about the countryside playing a thousand knavish tricks there, and in the convents of nuns, seizing whatever he thought fit to take. As I had already resolved to go on with my campaign against the President, be sure that I went off towards the village where he was sleeping, thinking he was as safe as the King in Madrid. I gave him a morning serenade and found him in bed; but he flung himself out of the window into a garden. But there were others who jumped as well as he did and fished him out again. They bound him, and I took him to the city of Aquila, where all the people were thunderstruck that anyone should have been found brave enough to seize him. I put him in the castle and tried him, and when this was done I gave him two days' grace, during which I occupied myself with having a scaffold put up in the midst of the market-place, and preparing knives for the sacrifice. The people laughed when they saw the scaffold, and heard that it was to cut off his head. But they were quite amazed when, on the fifth day, at three in the afternoon, they saw him without a head, which was cut off by a bad executioner, to whom I gave a suit of mine and ten crowns. The poor creature had not a practised hand; but he was like the doctors who give lessons in the hospitals at the expense of innocent people – though this gentleman was no innocent, but an arrant rogue. His name was Jacomo Ribera, and anyone in the Abruzzi would know him if only by name. And he was a native of the city of Aquila.

I stayed in this city over the Feast of the Resurrection, but the town councillors, or *regidores* (who fixed the prices of food), were on bad terms with me, because I would not let them live as they liked. So on Easter Day they thought they would find some pretext for not accompanying me to church and so would cause me some annoyance. I had told them on Holy Thursday that they were to receive the communion as I did, but they, being filled with perversity, would not do so. Easter Day came round, when the Bishop was to say pontifical High Mass. I waited until Mass was begun and went there, taking my place in my seat with nobody but my clerk – though he would never sign any of the sentences I have mentioned; but this did not alarm me, for he belonged to the place, and had to go on living there. You should know that in this city the magistrates or *regidores*, who are five in number, have each two attendants paid by the city, who are dressed in red; and none of these *regidores* or councillors will go outside his house without these two attendants, nor will he go elsewhere, even if it is a matter of life or death.

When I found myself alone at pontifical Mass and saw those ruffians' trick, I summoned the sergeant from where I sat and said to him, 'Go and arrest all the magistrates' attendants, and place six soldiers in the house of each magistrate, with orders to eat everything they can find in the house or the kitchen – observing the greatest respect towards the women – and not to leave the house till I tell them.' This was carried into effect at once, the more so because there were some soldiers who, because it was Easter Day, had had no fire lit in their houses. The councillors heard what was going on; but since they had not got their attendants with the red capes, they could not possibly manage to go home by themselves. They sent chamberlains and messages. I said they were to come in person. But since they could not come, each one stopped at the place where the sergeant had arrested his attendants. The Bishop begged me to remove the soldiers from the houses, or to let the attendants go, so that the councillors might go home. I granted that the soldiers should leave the houses on being given three testoons each, which is equal to nine reals. They paid them on the spot, and would have paid three hundred ducats not to see them in their houses. So greatly do they love us! And so the soldiers and their wenches had a finer Easter feast – what with their nine reals each and a dinner – than the councillors; for the latter had to celebrate the feast in whatever place their attendants were arrested; since they would not go to their own houses, lest they might lose their usage or privilege. The Bishop pressed me to set free the red capes. I said that I had arrested the attendants of all of them, so that they should not all make excuses as to which of them was to have carried my cushion and placed it in the church. But if each of them would pay a ducat to the House of Penitents, I would set the attendants at liberty. They paid up on the spot, and the councillors were set free from the spell, for such they had found it. A thousand other little incidents arose between me and them. One of these was that they fixed high prices for fish and meat, as well as bread, in return for which each of them received so much in kind of fish and meat; but their commission on bread was paid in money. I found this out, and told them that when they came to assess the prices, they were to consult me. They did so; and while they were making the assessment, I said, 'Does not your lordship see that it is a shame to put the price so low? For it is worth more, and if you raise the price, the supply will be more abundant.' They thought they saw the heavens opening, and put it up still higher. As soon as the assessment was made, I said to each of them, 'Gentlemen, my household consists of so many. But though I am exempt, in virtue of my position as a knight of Malta and captain of infantry and Military Governor and Governor, I wish to start paying the prices you have assessed. But each of your lordships must likewise buy provisions in proportion to his household, and pay on the spot, as I do; and I vow to God that if you shopkeepers give their lordships an ounce of anything free, I will have you flogged.' And when they saw that I meant it, they did as I had said. The councillors would say, 'But, sir, in our house we do not eat fish.' 'Then I wish you to eat it, and enjoy the fixed prices, as I and the poor do.' This sufficed to send the fixed prices down by a half and more for all commodities.

To return to our President, or Viceroy of the province, he had sent the last letter I wrote him to the Count of Monterey; so the Count resolved to take me away from Aquila, at the instance of the President and councillors. But he removed both him and me on the same day. He gave me a company of cuirassiers before I left Aquila, but he gave him nothing. Such was the end of my governorship of Aquila, which I held for three months and seven days.

Chapter xvii

Of Divers Things which happened to me in Capua.
In Praise of the Count and Countess of Monterey. I retire from their Service

‿

I LEFT Aquila for Naples to take possession of a
company of cavalry. I found it quartered at
Capua, and was forced to remove it to Naples,
where it was handed over to me by Don Gaspar
de Acevedo, General of a thousand cavalry.

On the day Don Gaspar de Acevedo handed it
over to me, in the presence of Don Pedro Cuncubi-
lete, clerk of the rations, an inventory was made of
the horses belonging to the company, which had
been under the command of Don Hector Pinatelo,
before his promotion to be Deputy-Quartermaster-
General. One of the soldiers said that a different
horse had been given back to him, and others said
the same; so I said to Don Hector, 'The horse your
Lordship is riding belongs to the company, and the
soldiers say that your Lordship has kept the best
horses, and given them the worst; and they are
the King's property.' 'It is not true,' he replied,

'I have not taken a single horse.' Now it is true that, among Italians, it is not an insult to say, 'It is not true.' Still, I did not want any slur upon my honour, for there were many Spaniards and Italians present; so at these words I raised my hand and, seizing the tip of his beard, I gave it a jerk. He dropped his stick, and drew his sword, like a gentleman of spirit. But I was not slow to draw my old blade; and we fought it out then and there, but without drawing blood, for there was such a crowd that it was impossible for us to wound each other. A poor German in the Viceregal Guard, who was standing by, had to pay the piper, for he got a slash in the face, as if he had been the one who pulled Don Hector's beard.

We were arrested by Don Gaspar de Acevedo, as General of Cavalry and Captain of the Guard to the Count of Monterey. Each of us was confined to his house under guard for three days, until the Count my master, after hearing the report of the Quartermasters and the Prince of Ascoli, ordered us to make it up in his antechamber. Don Hector was supported by the Prince of La Rochela and I by Señor Don Gaspar de Acevedo, but from that time onward we both went about – or rather

I did – with our eyes peeled, as the bravos say.

So now I was a captain of cavalry. But upon this fresh troubles began, chiefly because the Count my master desired to hold a general review of all the cavalry of the realm, and of the new levies – amounting to more than two thousand five hundred cavalry, with the Spanish and Italian infantry, which was numerous and most brilliant. For at this review there were to be present none of the unmounted militia of the realm, but only the regular levies, two thousand seven hundred Spaniards and eight thousand Italians, all picked men.

But what fine clothes we should need that day! For even I, poor as I was, displayed my two trumpeters and four lackeys in livery, all in scarlet, encrusted with silver lace, with gilded swords and sword-belts, and plumes and cloaks to match over their liveries.

And my horses, for I had five of them, with their saddles; two with silver lace and all with inlaid pistols in their saddle-bows! I sported arms of azure with silver flames, chamois-leather breeches encrusted with gold lace, with sleeves and collar to match, a crest of plumes, blue, green and white, upon my helmet; and a crimson scarf richly embroidered with gold. And upon my word it might have been used for a bedspread. In this array I entered the *plaza*, with my ensign and standard and eighty well-equipped horsemen behind me. The soldiers wore their red scarves, and my brother, who was my lieutenant, brought up the rear, all gallant and fine. You can imagine in what style we entered — [1]

I and the rest of the captains — and there were numbers of them — all defiled in front of the Palace, where there were standing on a balcony the Count my master, and Their Eminences the Cardinals Sabeli and Sandoval; and on another balcony my lady the Countess of Monterey and her ladyship the Marchioness of Monterroso with her ladies. As all the companies came on to the parade-ground one after the other, they made their horses caracole and lowered their standards, and the infantry their flags. They defiled along the whole length of the castle, where they formed into a squadron, and we had a sham fight; and a sight it was indeed to see the cavalry engaging the infantry. By this time Their Excellencies had already gone on with the lord Cardinals to Castelnuovo, and as they passed

[1] Line missing in the text.

by all the artillery was discharged, which was a
grand sight. And this was done so smartly that all
that was lacking was the shot, for the drill was carried
out in every detail. But we had such a Captain-
General that we could not have failed in it; for
though he had been nurtured all his life in war, he
could not have given the word of command better
than he did, nor more exactly at the right moment.
And this is no flattery; for I warrant you that,
though I have known any number of Princes, I
have never seen one who could keep up such a high
style as this lord. And if anyone try to say a word
to the contrary, let me recall his embassy extraordinary to Rome in 1628, and the grandeur in
which he lived there; the many guests whom I have
known to be lodged in his house – the lord Cardinals
Sandoval, Espínola and Albornoz, a brother of the
Count of Elda and another of the Count of Tavara,
and the wife of the same Count, and my lady the
Countess; and all of them would dine apart in their
own rooms, at the same time, yet there was no disorder in the service, nor among the pastry-cooks,
the butlers, the cooks and the plate; for each one
had whatsoever was necessary for him. Besides this,
each one had a valet and a chambermaid, and there

were coaches for them all at the same time, without having to beg any loans of anybody. I have seen thirty-two apartments hung with their summer draperies; and there were as many for the winter.

It was this lord who in OCTOBER, 1629, held such notable feasts at the birth of our Lord the Prince — whom God preserve! – that even to-day the Romans have not stopped talking about them, nor have the strangers who were present there. Such plays, such jousts, such fireworks, such fountains of wine, such alms given to the hospitals, such quantities of money, both gold and silver, scattered by handfuls in the evening for three days in succession. And if more proof be needed, it is enough to recall that at that time we were in such ill repute at Rome as can hardly be imagined; and yet such magnificence sent the people crowding into Rome, shouting, 'Viva España!' What more need I say?

Or again, who in that city has had so many led captains as the Count, at thirty crowns a month each? There were four of us, and I was one of them, and he paid us punctually out of his own pocket. All this was managed by Gaspar de Rosales, His Excellency's treasurer, who never gave cause for anyone to complain of His Excellency at that court.

The same was made Secretary of State and for War at Naples by His Excellency when he became Viceroy, an office well deserved by the good secretary for his vigilance and his clean hands. And sure it is that a master often succeeds through having a good servant, and fails for the lack of one.

Or again, what Viceroy has there been at Naples who has sought out men of merit, who were mewed up in despair in some castle, but His Excellency sought them out and rewarded them? And I know of many such. So all the nation rejoiced at seeing him honoured. Who but the Count has sent to Milan, in fifteen months, two regiments of Italians, of as much as three thousand men, and seven hundred thousand ducats; and to Spain six thousand infantry, and a thousand cavalry in twenty-four galleons? The infantry was under the command of the Marquis of Campo Lataro, and the cavalry under that of the Prince of La Rochela; and with them were twenty-four saddles, and embroidered bridles for their choice horses, and as many pairs of pistols beyond price; and on the back of each horse a covering of brocade descending to the fetlocks. This was sent as a present to His Majesty and His Highness the Infante Carlos, who is in glory, and to His Highness the Infante Cardinal. And then to speak of my lady the Countess: the affability which she showed towards all the titled ladies of the realm, dividing the days of the week between the hospitals, and going and serving with her own hands in the hospital for women, bringing from the Palace all the food which was to be used on that day. And to this I can bear witness. And what of the convent for rescued Spanish women which she founded? And others which she aids every day by her charity, showing favour and patronage to all those who would avail themselves of her intercession. In short, reader, let it not seem that I have spoken in passion, for I have fallen very short of their deserts; and I swear by God and by this cross ✠ that at the moment I write this, which is FEBRUARY 4, 1633, I am in Palermo, in disgrace with the Count my master, of which you will hear anon the why and the wherefore. But for all that, I esteem it more highly to be his servant, even in disgrace, than to be the servant of another, and in favour. For never will I be ungrateful for the favours received in his house, and his bread which I have eaten.

To return to my story: I was saying, sir, that our sham fights came to an end, and it was on the

20th of JUNE, 1632. We went back home tired and sweating, and on the morrow the Count ordered that all the cavalry should be distributed along the coasts to defend them, for warning had arrived of the Turkish fleet. It fell to my lot to go with five hundred horse, as chief of the troop, to the principality of Citra, where I remained till the end of August in the region of Bol (Eboli) and Achierno (Acerno). In this town I spent the dog-days, but it was so cold that I had to put two coverlets on my bed. And so by day we exercised the horses, skirmishing among ourselves, and at times tilting at the ring.

There was a great horse in the company, a four-year-old, and he was so vicious that he had almost lamed four soldiers, and one he had quite lamed. And in order to shoe him, it was necessary to bind his fore and hind legs; and he was so savage that if he were thrown on the ground, he would break every rope, however thick it might be. I ordered that he should be taken to the convent of our lord Saint Francis and given to it as an offering. They led him there without harness, and the guardian said that, since I was presenting him as an offering, would I give them a deed of gift, so that they might sell him? That night the horse was so savage that they did not dare to take him to drink. On the next day I made out the deed of gift, and the guardian said to me, 'Sir, I fear this horse may kill one of the brothers.' He went back with his deed to the monastery; and on the next day he said to me, 'Sir Captain, the horse has become quiet, and seems to be a little steadier.' In short, within six days he became so tame that no donkey could be tamer, and they harnessed him with a mare which belonged to the convent, and he went in harness with her as if he were not a horse, so that the whole town marvelled. I had a horse among others that was called Colona. And as we went to joust and sham-fight every day in the avenue of San Francisco, one day I mounted this horse, which was a quiet one, and I had often used him for sham-fighting and jousting with the lance. But when I tried to make him start, nothing would move him. I was angry and gave him the spur, and he started; but after four paces he stopped. I turned him back to the starting-point, and he did the same. He would only go a very little way, and that sideways. They asked me to dismount and retire from the joust. One of the soldiers said to me, 'Let your worship give him to me; for I will make him go, and he will be rid of this vice.' I dismounted and the soldier got on his back. But he had hardly mounted, when the horse shot off at a gallop, and did not stop till he had dashed into a wall, both he and the soldier together; and they both fell down dead, at which I stood thunderstruck. Either it was due to the offering that I had made of the horse, or to an altar which I had set up to say Masses for the souls in Purgatory, and a brief which I had obtained for them from Rome so that the altar should be privileged. What the cause was, God knows, to Whom I give thanks for this grace, with many others which He grants me daily.

I entered Naples with my company, and was given quarters at the bridge of La Maddalena, whence I went forth every night with twenty horsemen to patrol the shore of Torre del Greco, and the other companies did the same on the other side, towards Pozzuoli.

I had very fine horses, but the companies of my troop were not good. So, in order to reorganize them, the Count gave orders that my company should be disbanded, which was done; and His Excellency granted me the honour of the governorship of Pescara, which is among the best in that realm. I kissed the Count's hand for this favour, and remained for more than a month without asking for my patent. One morning the Count my master sent word to me by the Secretary Rosales that he would be glad for me to make ready two small galleons and a patache which were in the harbour, and go with them to the Levant to hunt the pirates a little.

At this time I had with me a brother who had served His Majesty for twenty years, in Italy and in the Royal Armada, as soldier, sergeant and ensign, and as governor of a company for three years, with a general's commission, and eight crowns' extra pay for the King's special service; and he had just been discharged with the rank of a lieutenant of cuirassiers. I said to the Secretary, 'Sir, I will do as the Count commands. But let your worship consider that I have my brother, and let him at least remain at Pescara as my deputy.' He told me this could not be, for the man who held that post must be a captain. I begged that he might be made captain of the patache, and I even begged it of the Count by word of mouth; but he would not do it. I asked if he might be given a company made up of the scattered bands and light troops who were to embark with me; and they consented. In the meanwhile I was at work fitting out the ships, and I said to the secretary, 'Your worship, do not mock me. Ask the Count to settle this once for all. I swear to God that if he does not, I shall refuse to sail or go on the expedition.' And so we went on, till one night, in his office, he undeceived me, saying that nothing would be given my brother, but that we were to sail together. Upon this I went home and thought things over: how I had no command in that realm, nor pay from His Majesty, nor had my brother. And my brother kept saying, 'Sir, I have served as everybody knows, and your worship has done services to many people, and yet I can find no advancement. The world will think that there is something against me.' I saw that he was right, and was moved to collect my few belongings and place them in the convent of the Most Holy Trinity. And from thence I wrote a memorial to the Secretary, the tenor of which was as follows:

'Let not your worship be amazed that I have been importunate in seeking a place for my brother; for since I had to go on this expedition, he would have been left, in case of my decease, with our little nephew and niece upon his hands, who are orphans, and have no father but me. But since your worship last night took away from me all hope that something would be given him, I have resolved that I will not serve either, nor go on this voyage. So your worship may say to the Count my master that I have retired hither, to consider where I may decide to go and earn my living; and lest Your Excellency may imprison me in a fortress in a fit of anger. If the Count be pleased that I should serve him and go on this voyage, let him give a company to my brother, since he deserves it, and it had been promised to me. And I will come forth at once and make this voyage, and do what deeds you shall see.'

The Secretary was amazed to see such determination and wrote me a letter as man to man, asking me to come out. But I refused to do so, except on the above-mentioned terms.

I asked leave of the Count for myself and for my brother and nephew. He sent me word that I had no need of his leave, since I was not his subject, being a knight of Malta, and having no pay or occupation in that realm; and that a certificate from the board of health was sufficient. I sent word to him that I was not one to go off without leave from the place where I had been employed. That if His Excellency did not grant it me, I would remain there in the convent until I died, or His Excellency was promoted to a higher office. And so His Excellency did me the favour of granting me special leave to go to Malta, and to my brother for Spain, and to my nephew for Sicily; and he sent me all three of them to the convent, signed with his own hand.

Afterwards, when the ships were about to start, I was sent a letter from the Palace, signed by the Secretary – but it was from another and a higher quarter – in which I was ordered to draw up a description, or instruction, as to the way in which the ships were to be managed. I did so, in the presence of him who brought the letter; and it was very long, and at the end of it I said, 'Sir, I am no angel, and I may err. So let this instruction he laid before the pilots. And if my opinion seem good, let it be used; but if not, let it not be used. For this was the voyage I was thinking of making, had I not had the misfortune to have brothers.'

I next turned my attention to the arrangements for my journey; though every one told me I ought to wait, even ministers and my friends in the Palace. I endeavoured to take counsel with them; and I even resolved one night to go and see the Secretary Rosales at the Palace. I did so, and remained a long time talking with him. He told me that I had not acted wisely, so we left it that I was to see him another night. But I did not think fit to do so. I took a felucca, which cost me much good money, and put my brother and nephew on board her at dead of night, with the little gear which I possessed. And we left Naples on the 20th of JANUARY, at midnight.

I forgot to say that, owing to my retirement into that monastery, everybody thought I had turned monk – as if I had not already taken vows. It was even put in the *Gazette*, and they wrote to me from Malta that they had heard I was a Capuchin. It was not surprising that they should say this in distant lands, for during the two months I stayed in that monastery there was a man actually in Naples who swore he had seen me say Mass. But he could not have known that I do not know Latin, nor do I even understand it.

DE CONTRERAS

I passed those two months there doing penance, with a capon in the morning and another at night, and other trifles, and with very good old wine; and I heard four Masses and vespers daily.

The night I left Naples was not a very happy one, on account of the anxiety of my mind. But at daybreak we were at Bietre (Vietri), sixty miles from Naples. We crossed the Gulf of Salerno and came to Palanudo (Cape Palinuro), where we were not allowed to land because of the quarantine. From thence we went to Paola, and I stayed there two days. I visited the birthplace of the blessed St. Francis of Paola. From thence I passed to Castillon, where I met a felucca bound for Naples. It bore a fine Spanish lady of my acquaintance, with whom I supped that night, and she asked me to sleep in her room, for she was afraid. I did not wish to be ungracious, and so I lay down in her room in the other bed.

Day broke, and we launched our feluccas; and each went on its chosen course. That night I arrived at Tropia (Tropea), but I did not pass the night there, and pushed on, arriving at Messina on Christmas Eve, which we passed at an inn where there was wantonness and to spare. But since it was Christmas Eve everybody kept quiet, and I in particular, who had taken my fill before coming there.

We heard Mass on the feast-day, or rather many Masses, and we left Messina. But we could not get past the lighthouse, and here we slept.

On the morrow we went aground, and laboured with our oars as far as Melaço (Milazzo), where we lay a night and a day, on account of bad weather. The captain-at-arms presented me with some fowls and wine and a kid, so that my larder was replenished and we had a grand feast at the inn. For in such houses there is never any lack of devils, both male or female.

We left Milazzo and, without touching land, we were borne on as far as Termines (Termini), where there is good lodging. We slept here and left for Palermo, arriving at midday. Here I found endless numbers of friends, and busied myself with setting up house. But before doing this I spoke to the lord Duke of Alcalá, who is governor of this realm. I told him how I had come, but His Excellency knew all about it. And I besought him to give order that they should settle with me about the thirty crowns' maintenance money due to me in this realm from His Majesty. He at once gave orders that this should be done.

My brother sent in a memorial, entreating His Excellency, in consideration of his services, to do him the honour of conferring on him a captain's commission to go and raise a company, for there were but few in that realm. I gave him five hundred ducats for this purpose, which is the amount given by His Majesty for these levies; for I wished to save the King this sum. The reply was that inquiry should be made in the department concerned. And the verdict was, that he be placed on board a tartan which was lying in the harbour – a Catalan boat, with a cargo of biscuit for the galleys of that realm – which was going to Genoa. I gave him two hundred golden crowns and his clothes, and paid for the hire of the boat and purchase of stores, and gave him my blessing, saying, 'My son, go you to Flanders, and there you will become a captain. You carry with you your record, fine clothes, money and leave of absence. May God guide you!' Upon which he went off in God's keeping, and here I have stayed till to-day, the 4th of FEBRUARY, 1633, when I am writing this. If God grant me life, and anything else happen, I will add it in this place.

Chapter xviii

Voyages to Naples, Genoa and Spain. My Brother's Pretensions

ဏ

WHEN my brother had gone off in the year '33 in the aforesaid tartan, I stayed at Palermo; and my lord Duke of Alcalâ, who was Viceroy of Sicily, sent and summoned me. I went up to see him, and he asked me what had happened between me and the Count of Monterey. I told him nothing, but that I had the Count's leave to go to Malta. He pressed me with questions. But I never told him anything of what had happened to me in Naples. I took leave of His Excellency, and went down to the guard-room, and the captains began to cross-question me again as to what had happened between me and the Count at Naples. I told them to let the Count be, for though he was a little man he was the master of all the grandees. There were not lacking those who went off and told this to the Duke of Alcalâ, who was vexed, and sent word to his secretary to summon me. As soon as I arrived, he said to me without more ado, 'Your worship is to pay Don Jeronimo de Castro the two hundred crowns you owe him.' And there was present the said Don Jeronimo de Castro. 'Sir,' I replied to the Secretary, 'it is true that he gave me two hundred crowns, to obtain a facultative brief for him in Rome for the Grand Master of Malta. But the said Grand Master would not sanction the brief, so that I have done with my part of the business.' 'Your worship,' replied the said Secretary, 'you have nothing to say for yourself. You must pay at once, or your person will be seized.' Seeing his resolute bearing, I replied, 'Let your worship send some one with me to fetch them.' He sent me under guard, and I brought them in a bag, and said to him, 'Let your worship take and give them to the Duke to do as he likes with them, provided none of them are given to Don Jeronimo de Castro.' On this I went back to my lodging, musing on the ways of the world. Two days later he sent a sergeant-major's adjutant, who told me that His Excellency's orders were to settle with me about the maintenance money awaiting me there. I answered that I was drawing no pay there, but that I had leave from the Count of Monterey to go to Malta. Upon which I was forced to apply to the Collector of the Order, and ask him to speak to the Viceroy. He did so, and then I was left in peace. Within twenty days I received from Malta the bulls conferring on me the commandery of St. John at Puente de Orbi, which had been assigned to me. I abode there two months. During this time there came two galleys from Genoa, bearing with them a Bishop. I asked the captain of one of them if he were willing to take me to Naples, on condition that he did not tell the Count he was taking me. He agreed to do so; but the first thing he did was to tell him. The Count already knew, through the Gazettes, all that had taken place in Sicily. He sent for his Secretary, Gaspar de Rosales, and told him to send and summon me, and try to get hold of me and keep me in Naples. The Secretary sent me a curt, brief letter to the galley, in which he said, 'The Count has had word in advance that your worship is coming here. Come and dine with me, for we have a bone to pick together.' Seeing that I needs must, I landed from the galley and came to the Palace, where I had an interview with the Secretary and showed my bulls. He was quite taken aback, and went upstairs to show them to the Count, who said, 'Contreras has something to turn aside wrath! Cross-question him, upon my life! so that he stays here on shore.' We dined, and they lectured me well, so that I had no option but to stop. The two galleys were just departing to Gaeta, where others were awaiting them to go to Genoa. The Secretary gave me a packet from the Count to give into the hand of the Marchioness of Charela in person. I did so, and the gun had already given the signal to weigh anchor, when the Governor of Gaeta sent an armed brigantine to fetch me to Naples. But all my gear was at the bottom of everything and could not be got out, and they were already taking the cargo on board, so I took advantage of this. We made a prosperous voyage to Genoa, where we arrived, and two days later came the Cardinal Infante – may his soul rest in glory! He made a brave entry, and from thence he went off to Milan, and I towards Spain in the galleys which had brought the Cardinal Infante. I arrived at Barcelona in a short space and went from thence to Madrid, where I took lodgings in the house of Secretary Juan Ruiz de Contreras, the father of Don Fernando, who is now at the top of the tree. He entertained me well in his house, and I began to busy myself with my claims. The first thing to do was to go and take possession of my commandery.

I returned to Madrid, and came upon my brother, who was also a suitor, begging to be granted the pay due to him when he was discharged from his post in Flanders. When his claim had gone before the Council, he was given twenty crowns' maintenance money and a letter to the office of the Secretary Rojas recommending him for a company. Rojas sent a note to the Secretary Pedro de Arce informing him of this favour. But he referred it to the councillors of State, and dragged the matter out for days by insinuating to them that I had been a sham captain of cavalry, and that he was not bound to give me this commission. I heard of this after a few days. As my brother's affair was not dealt with, I went to the Marquis of Santa Cruz, of the Council of State, and pressed him on the subject; so he replied, 'How can you expect your brother's commission to be given him? Why, Pedro de Arce says that your worship was a sham cavalry captain.' On which I turned my back on the Marquis without saying anything, and went back home. And without eating a mouthful, I got out my commission as captain in the cuirassiers, and the other as chief of a troop of five hundred, and my discharge and leave of absence; and I hurried off on foot to the

EXCELL^{mo} D^{no} DON ALVAR BAZAN MARCH DE Sta CRVC CATH
MA A STAT CONSIL ET CVBICVL OCEAN QVACVNQ HISP. MONARCH DOMI
PROPR Æ P BELGIOR ARM PER BELG. GVBERN

PONTIUS, AFTER VAN DYCK: THE MARQUIS OF SANTA CRUZ
(British Museum, Print Room)

house of the Marquis of Santa Cruz. I was admitted, and said to him, 'I beseech Your Excellency to hear me. More than twenty years ago I was at the Postern of San Martín, when a lady called me up late at night. I went upstairs, and we stayed talking for a while, when there was again a knocking at the gate. The lady told me to hide myself, and Pedro de Arce – for it was he who had come – would soon go away. I said that I had no cause to hide myself; but let him be admitted. The lady, in distress, gave orders to admit him. Up came Señor Pedro de Arce with his rapier and buckler, as green as a lettuce. He was then an official of the Council of War. As soon as he saw me, he asked me what I was doing there. I answered, 'This lady was inquiring about a friend of hers.' But, without letting me finish my sentence, he raised his buckler. I was ready for him, and was so quick that I gave him a thrust, so that he, the buckler and the rapier rolled downstairs, he yelling that he was murdered, though he was not even wounded.

'I came down too, under cover of the confusion, and made off, with God's help. But he was carried home half dead from his fall, so that ever since that time he has had a spite against me. And now Your

Excellency sees this commission, leave of absence, and discharge, from which you will see, once and for all, that what has been told you is not true, but that I was a captain of cuirassiers for seven months and three days.'

(Here ends the MS. A few pages of it are missing, which may have taken the story down to the year 1640. It has been impossible to ascertain the date at which Alonso de Contreras died. In the archives of the parish church of San Sebastian, at Madrid, are to be found entries of the deaths of two persons with the same Christian and surnames: one, married to Ana de Urosa, died on JUNE 29, 1637; the other, whose wife was Maria de la Cuadra, on DECEMBER 29, 1653. Both of them were buried by charity. Señor Serrano y Sanz, from whose edition of the original manuscript, first made for the Royal Historical Academy of Madrid, this translation has been made, believes that neither of them is the author of the present autobiography, though he thinks it by no means impossible, especially at that period, that the wheel of Fortune should have taken such a turn.)

Appendix i

Epistle Dedicatory of 'El Rey Sin Reino,' by
Lope Felix de Vega Carpio

To Captain Alonso de Contreras, Knight of the
Military Order of St. John

Had you been born at Rome, Sir Captain, in the
golden centuries of her domination, when she was
head of the world in arms, you would not, I think,
have failed to win a crown, such as they were wont
to grant to soldiers of valour for heroic deeds;
crowns mural, naval, or triumphal. Much honour
is done to Madrid, your worship's birthplace, and
to those of us who are natives of her, in that you,
who left her arms at such a tender age, and were
thrown, as it were, upon the mercy of Fortune,
should have won, by your own arm, such high
renown, such honourable offices, and that white cross
which adorns your breast with no worldly order by
its side. All these bear witness unexceptionable and
beyond all doubt, in the eyes of those to whom
worth is measured by merit, of how high was the
courage by which they were won. A worthy subject

for an extended history or heroic poem would be your innumerable mighty deeds, from the day on which your worship first proved your sword at Patras, a town in Turkey, and justified your hopes by your brave exploits. For the very sea appeared to bow and obey you, who, surmounting its perils and subduing its billows, won in a few voyages, with a single frigate, armed by the Grand Master's nephew, more than three hundred captives. And so throughout the whole of Barbary the Spaniard of Malta was dreaded, and his name was famous and held in peculiar renown. What pen would not be proud to write of your voyage in the galleon of Captain Pedro Betrián, when you captured the Turk Axema in valiant combat? Or the ship in the port of the Venetians, where, since they were promised ten crowns for every Turk, a hundred soldiers leapt ashore. And after many a mighty deed, that brave Turk fell to your worship's sword – he who with pike aslope and on it an orange pennon, with barbarous words hurled defiance at the nations; but you, with sword and buckler alone, took him captive; you took from him the flag, and defended it likewise from some French soldiers who claimed a share of what they had not won. And when the

slaves were shared out, a hundred crowns, in addition
to your other rewards, were given to your worship
for the flag, with the honour of wearing it on your
arms when such should be granted you; for there
are no arms in the world more noble than those
which a man wins with his own sword.

But who could tell of the dauntless valour with
which, in a single frigate, by order of the new
Grand Master, your worship spied out the fleet of
Soliman at Negropont, and gave warning to my
lord Rutinel, Governor of Reggio, that they were
coming to take the place? For which cause he
bravely laid an ambush at the Fossa di San Giovanni
and cut the throats of three hundred Turks, capturing seventy and four. Or that feat by which you
crossed over through the midst of the fleet to give
warning to the cities of Taormina and Syracuse,
when your leg was pierced by a musket-shot, and
three of your soldiers were killed. And when you
arrived at Malta, it was held of such importance
that the Grand Master was forewarned. So Soliman
returned without honour, and with heavy losses
from among his janissaries. Or who should paint
that famous day of St. Gregory, when the slaves
fled from Malta; but your worship followed them

and overtook them, and conquered them and brought them back with the plunder they had stolen? Or who should tell of your voyage to the Nile, and the ambuscade of fifteen hundred Moors on their way to Mecca, in which you showed yourself as brave as you were fortunate? Who should tell of the information which you brought from all those coasts, bringing back seventeen Turks to Malta from Tripoli in Syria? Who should tell of the careenage of Chios, where Soliman of Catania, who was afterwards King of Algiers, kept his best-beloved wife, a Hungarian by race and peerless in beauty? But you took her and bore her away with other slaves. And when he followed you with two galleys to St. John of Patmos, you freed yourself by your skill in war, where force would have been of no avail. Or what shall I say of the courage you showed when you won Pasaba, that strong fortress? Or what of your service at La Mahometa, above all when you won your way by swimming to the frigate, thus saving your life; till the Grand Master granted you leave for Spain, and His Majesty, after your varying fortunes, bestowed on you the favour of Captain Don Pedro de Jaraba's colours? Or what of that later time when you were captain of the Duke of Feria's two galleons, in which you did such notable deeds at Cyprus and Alexandria, and returned with the prize of that English galleon, which for three years had been a famous pirate throughout the whole Ocean? Or again, your great travail in Spain, and the late expedition to Flanders, where you served for three years with so much valour, and gave satisfaction on all occasions. Or your prison in Burgundy, after the death of Henry IV, and your adventures at Lyons, which is in France, until you returned to Malta; where, in spite of envy and persecution, you received the habit, which might have borne upon its hem: 'I act; I do not ask.' Likewise your relief of the islands of Barlovento (Windward Islands). Or that of La Mámora, so great a service on such a critical occasion. But why should I attempt to number in one letter what many books could not possibly contain? Forgive this hardihood, due to my love, which I confess is great, but firmly grounded in your worth and valour. For, as I said at the beginning, starting with neglect from your country, you took Fortune by the forelock, and have arrived by the work of your own hands at the place which you now hold; and your life now being freed from so many disputes, assaults, battles, ambuscades, jealousies, challenges, seas, and strange lands – and finally twice from poison – I can only tell your worship that, if mine does not fail me, I hope to have the honour of writing at length in uplifted verse your deeds of valour, not envying those whose pen was employed on those of Garcia de Paredes, Urbina and Céspedes, those famous Spaniards, who by their illustrious deeds consecrated their country and their renown to immortality. Meantime let your worship accept these words as an earnest and take this comedy under your protection.

Your worship's servant, friend and chaplain,

LOPE FELIX DE VEGA CARPIO

Appendix ii

Memorial drawn up by Contreras, now in the Archives at Simancas (General Archives of Simancas: Grace and Justice; Military Services, Dossier 2, Folio 56)

SIR,

Captain Alonso de Contreras, of the military order of St. John, states that he has served Your Majesty continuously for twenty-eight years in Italy, Malta, Flanders, and the fleets, on every occasion which has offered itself, having been present at the capture of the cities of Pasaba and Mahometa and the expeditions to Tripoli and Algiers; and having been sent in particular several times to collect information in Turkey and Barbary about the enemy's fleet, where he had many encounters with them; and when he was in Turkey with his frigate, he had news that General Cigala was coming with all his fleet, intending to do much damage in Christian territory by taking the city of Reggio; but hastening ahead, he came and gave warning to the governor of the place, who laid an ambush, and, when they landed, slaughtered three hundred

Turks and took captive seventy-four, so that the
enemy was scattered without doing any harm; and
the said captain, being ordered to pass through the
midst of the fleet to give warning to the cities of
Taormina and Syracuse, was wounded on the way
thither by a musket-shot and lost nine soldiers; and
having come to Spain, Your Majesty sent him to
serve in Flanders, where he stayed till he received
the honour of a company of Spanish infantry in the
regiment of Quartermaster Don Pedro Estebán de
Ávila, with which he served till Your Majesty sent
him with two relief ships, bearing infantry and
munitions of war, to the Islands of Barlovento,
which were being molested by the enemy; and
having performed this service and returned to Spain
with fifty crowns a month, he was told to betake
himself to Cadiz to salve the remains of the Philippine fleet, and was especially ordered to go to the
Strait of Gibraltar and fetch twenty pieces of bronze
artillery, which they heard that the enemy's ships
desired to carry off — his orders being to avoid
engaging them, but if they forced him to do so and
he found himself overpowered, that he should sink
his ship and give orders to the other ships which he
took with him to do the same, so that the enemy

should not make use of the artillery; and he shipped it and brought it to the city of Cadiz; and while he was there, news came that La Mámora was besieged by sea and by land; and since nobody would volunteer to take them reinforcements of infantry and munitions and to reconnoitre the bar, he offered to do it, and went off, being instructed to land the reinforcements or allow himself to be cut to pieces; but within twenty-six hours he arrived and landed the said reinforcements, though he met two enemy ships which tried to molest him; and that same day the siege was raised on the land side, thanks to his relief; and within another twenty-six hours he returned to Spain, and took post-horses and came in haste to the Court in three days, spending the small savings he possessed, in order to relieve Your Majesty of the anxiety which he was in; for which Your Majesty ordered an official decree to be given him that the Council of the Indies should propose him for a place such as he aspired to; and finally Your Majesty ordered him to raise another company of infantry about the Court, which he did, with the integrity for which he is well known, raising two hundred and fifty-one soldiers for it; and he has served for a year in the fleet which guards the

Strait, and particularly in the encounter which it had with the Dutch, having embarked with his company in the Admiral of Naples, which was one of those in action that day; and he has likewise brought up three more brothers to serve Your Majesty, who are still serving to-day, one in Flanders and another in Sicily, as ensigns without a command, another being a sergeant in the aforesaid company, and he has received no favours in return for all these services.

In consideration of all this, and of the fact that Don Juan Fajardo disposed of his company to another person, though he came with a commission; and that Your Majesty has ordered by his royal warrant that it should be returned to him, in spite of the fact that it has already been disposed of; and that the secretary Martin Aroztegui has sent a remonstrance to the said Don Juan de Fajardo, but he has made no reply; and that the said captain is incapable of pleading against a general, and is ruined, though he only desires to serve.

He entreats Your Majesty to grant him the boon of honouring him with one of the companies which are to be allotted at the expense of the Duke of

Tursi; for thus will he set free the thirty crowns'
pay with which Your Majesty honoured him for the
Atlantic fleet in the year 1620; and he will esteem
it a favour on the part of Your Majesty.

Appendix iii

Second Memorial on the same Subject

SIR,

Captain Alonso de Contreras states that, after his long service, having arrived at the city of Cadiz with a company of three hundred foot-soldiers which he raised at Court by order of Your Majesty, General Don Juan Fajardo dismembered it into eleven bands, and ordered him to embark with his colours on a tender with sixty men and to place himself under the orders of a caulker whom he had created sea-captain for this occasion – though he (Contreras) was the senior of all the infantry captains which were present; but so that he should not be reproached with complaining, which would have excused the way in which he was treated, he bore it for nine months, till they went into winter quarters, and put up with many other things to which he was subjected, by the said Don Juan Fajardo and the governor of these companies, in order to ruin him; and in order to avoid these disputes he asked for leave, and the answer was that, if he liked, he might leave his company, or else write a letter dated at

Seville on MARCH 2 – though it was then FEBRUARY
9 – in which he said that, since his health did not
improve, the said general might dispose of his company; but he only gave him this letter in order that
he might manage to get away on leave, in order to
come and complain to Your Majesty of the injuries
he had received; but by the same letter will be seen
the cunning with which he was treated, since, though
he had not been to Seville and presented himself
before the Secretary Martin de Arostegui on MARCH 1,
the letter is dated on the 2nd of the same at Seville;
and having besought Your Majesty to give orders
that his company should be transferred to the
Atlantic fleet, or wherever it might best serve Your
Majesty, orders were given to the said Don Juan
Fajardo to do so, in spite of the fact that he had
disposed of it; but he has delayed answering to this
effect for four months and has only now replied;
but since the petitioner does not know what state-
ments he may make, he begs to inform Your Majesty
that he has never given up his company, and has
always fulfilled his obligations; but not having
enough resources to plead against his generals, he
beseeches Your Majesty to order that he may be
granted one of the companies of the Duke of Tursi,

as head of it, and if there is no vacancy, that Your Majesty may employ him in his royal service, so that he may be far away from the said Don Juan Fajardo; and he will esteem it a favour on the part of Your Majesty.